DIALOGUE

For Bill —
My Best
Jack Spong

DIALOGUE

*In Search of
Jewish-Christian
Understanding*

John Shelby Spong
Jack Daniel Spiro

Prologue by FRANK EDWIN EAKIN, JR.

Christianity for the Third Millennium
and
St. Johann Press
HAWORTH, NJ

For further educational resources exploring the ideas and issues
addressed in this and other books by John Shelby Spong, contact:

Christianity for the Third Millennium
P.O. Box 69
Morristown, NJ 07963–0069
Fax: 973–540–9584
email: cmsctm@aol.com

Original publication: Seabury Press, Inc. 1975

Library of Congress Cataloging in Publication Data

Spong, John Shelby.
   Dialogue : In search of Jewish and Christian understanding

Bibliography.
   1. Judaism—Relations—Christianity 2. Christianity
and other religions—Judaism. I. Spiro, Jack D. joint
author. II. Title
BM 535.S686   261.2   75.2192
ISBN 1-878282-16-6

To
THE CONGREGATIONS OF
TEMPLE BETH AHABAH
AND
ST. PAUL'S EPISCOPAL CHURCH
RICHMOND, VIRGINIA

Called to seek the truth of God
Come whence it may
Cost what it will

CONTENTS

PREFACE

One never knows what will result from an unexpected telephone call, but in that manner this volume was conceived. As two clergymen, a priest and a rabbi, living within our different traditions in the same city, we each knew something of the other's public image, but had never met.

A recently published book changed these circumstances. The book was written by the priest, who sought to probe the ancient heritage of Christianity. In so doing, he expressed an unusual appreciation for the Jewish tradition as the foundation for the Christian claim about Jesus as the Christ. There appeared to the rabbi ample common ground in this book to make discussion stimulating, as well as sufficient disagreement to make debate real. So he called the author-priest, inviting him to public debate in the synagogue.

When we met to discuss the details, our conversations were rich, deep, and satisfying. The more we talked, the longer grew the proposed debate; and indeed debate itself faded into dialogue. We planned no special publicity in connection with this dialogue; it was originally for our local congregations only. We were thus surprised to discover that this quickly became the focus of community-wide attention. Every dialogue session was fully covered by the daily press. Front page stories sought to lay theological issues before the population of the metropolitan Richmond area. The holy name Yahveh was actually used in a headline, which was undoubtedly a first in Richmond history. Synagogue crowds at the dialogues were ten times the usual Sabbath eve services, while church attendance exceeded the previous Easter service. Virginia's largest radio station recorded the dialogues for presentation a month later. Richmond's educational television station asked us to repeat it live in a two-hour prime time broadcast. For two months the public forum column of the editorial page of the morning newspaper was filled with reader debate concerning the dialogues. Finally, community pressure demanded that the series be published, making this book a possibility.

We, a rabbi and a priest, had succeeded in bringing theological discussion into the real lives of a sizable number of people; and, in the process, we discovered a deep and abiding friendship. For this we are thankful.

We would like to express our thanks publicly to Dr. Frank Edwin Eakin, Jr., Associate Professor of Religion at the University of Richmond, who worked with us from the beginning, helping us to frame our questions and discover new dimensions heretofore hidden within our respective traditions. He also contributed the prologue, which set our dialogue in its historic context.

We would also like to acknowledge with special gratitude the support given us by the National Conference of Christians and Jews in sponsoring this volume both in Richmond and throughout the United States. The NCCJ has for years encouraged dialogue across the Jewish-Christian barrier. Though obviously the opinions expressed herein are our own, the NCCJ is nonetheless an appreciated partner in enabling this dialogue to become a model beyond this city.

There are many others without whom this book could not have been written and who deserve a special word of commendation and thanks from us:

Lucy Boswell Negus, the administrative assistant at St. Paul's, who shaped and corrected copy for the original dialogue as well as for this publication, bringing her special genius and poetic insight into much of the script.

Carter Donnan McDowell, who was our content editor, working especially on the birth narratives and who, along with Mrs. Negus, went to Clinton, Mass., for the final proofreading.

Robin Reeder Valentine, who both designed the cover and suggested many valuable changes in the text.

Frances Crockett Eakin, who originally contracted to be our typist but who became more than a typist has ever been, working with us until late at night, offering suggestions, clarifying sentences, and keeping us in good humor with both her wit and charm.

Edward Neal Hanchey, who did the art work that made the cover a reality.

Neil Keller Stutts, who was the photographer responsible for the picture appearing on the back cover.

Jean Leonard LeRoy, Pendleton Powell Carmody, and Cyane Hoar Lowden who did copy editing and assisted in many other ways.

Edward S. Hirschler, whose practical counsel and foresight helped to bring the idea for this book to fruition.

Finally, we each would like to pay tribute to those members of our respective families, who share with us our total life experience: to Joan Ketner Spong and daughters Ellen, Katharine, and Jaquelin; and to Marilyn Loevy Spiro and children Hillary, David, and Ellen. Without the love and concern of this special community in which we each live, life itself would not be near so sweet.

JACK DANIEL SPIRO
JOHN SHELBY SPONG

Richmond, Virginia
January 1975

CALL TO CHRISTIAN AND JEW

We can
build mutual appreciation of each tradition;
we can
affirm our unity in our origins;
we can
celebrate our common heritage;
we can
recognize the deep debt we each owe to the other.

There is a common humanity
that we share;
we are committed to our oneness and our holiness
as human beings, and for that
we can
thank Yahveh, our common God,
who is what he is
and will be what he will be
for all peoples.

Amen.

DIALOGUE

Prologue

SHALOM: *Faith's Quest, Man's Hope*

> *". . . they shall beat their swords into plowshares,*
> *and their spears into pruning hooks;*
> *nation shall not lift up sword against nation,*
> *neither shall they learn war any more"* [ISA. 2:4]

PARTICIPANTS IN THE LOCAL DIALOGUE

Fortuitous circumstances sometimes converge to bring together individuals of common presupposition and interest. The result frequently is an exciting interchange of ideas which potentially leaves all parties to the exchange broadened and enlightened in their perspectives. When such an exchange occurs between Jewish and Christian congregations, those individuals who affirm both faith perspectives are encouraged to enlarge their horizons and to be more understanding and appreciative of those persons affirming positions different from their own.

Such circumstances have brought together John S. Spong and Jack D. Spiro in Richmond, Virginia. Both of these men were born in the South during the early thirties, Spong in Charlotte, North Carolina, and Spiro in New Orleans, Louisiana; but in terms of background this may be the extent of their natal similarity. Mr. Spong was born into a family where a rigid, moralistic fundamentalism dominated, while Rabbi Spiro's background is Reform Judaism. As these two individuals made commitments to life vocations, however—one to the Christian ministry and the other to the rabbinate—a common type of pilgrimage was developing, a concern for truth, for openness, for

15

sharing faith's implications with others through any vehicle of communication which might be accessible.

Rabbi Spiro exemplifies the traditional Jewish love of learning, a trait that brought him to Tulane University, where he was awarded a Bachelor of Arts degree with honors, and then to Hebrew Union College in Cincinnati, where he earned the Master of Arts with honors and the Doctor of Hebrew Letters degrees. In 1967, following a six-year association as rabbi with the Anshe Emeth Memorial Temple in New Brunswick, New Jersey, he was appointed the national director of the Commission on Jewish Education of the Union of American Hebrew Congregations and the Central Conference of American Rabbis, a post he held until 1973. As the national director he was charged with the responsibility of giving leadership to the educational programs of Reform congregations in the United States plus the editorship of the union's books. As a productive scholar himself he is a contributing author to *Currents and Trends in Contemporary Jewish Thought*, edited by Benjamin Efron, and the textual author of the *Heritage Album*; he co-authored *The Living Bible* and authored *A Time to Mourn*, a study of the psychology of grief in Jewish tradition. In addition he has contributed articles to numerous journals, was earlier a visiting professor of Jewish education at the Hebrew Union College-Jewish Institute of Religion in New York City, and currently serves as an adjunct professor of religious studies at Virginia Commonwealth University in Richmond, Virginia. Quite obviously Rabbi Spiro is well equipped both by training as a Reform rabbi and as a productive scholar to speak authoritatively for the Jewish tradition.

No less secure is Mr. Spong's position as a spokesman for a liberal Christian perspective. His undergraduate work was taken at the University of North Carolina where he graduated with Phi Beta Kappa honors. His professional training was continued at Virginia Theological Seminary in Alexandria, Virginia, where he was awarded the Master of Divinity degree, with his ordination to the priesthood occurring in 1955. He served as rector of St. Joseph's Episcopal Church in Durham, North Carolina (1955–

1957), Calvary Episcopal Church in Tarboro, North Carolina (1957–1965), and St. John's Episcopal Church in Lynchburg, Virginia (1965–1969), prior to becoming the rector of St. Paul's Episcopal Church in Richmond, Virginia, in 1969. He has exercised considerable influence within the national Episcopal Church, having been appointed to numerous positions of leadership within the Church. In 1973 he was elected to membership on the Executive Council of the Episcopal Church. This post, which expires in 1979, is an assignment which comes to very few priests in their lifetime. It is a significant position in that a member of the Executive Council may influence national ecclesiastical policy; and, among other issues, Mr. Spong has advocated revision of *The Book of Common Prayer* and the updating of educational materials published by and used within the Church. His teaching concerns have been demonstrated in weekly adult Bible study classes conducted both in his parish at Lynchburg and at St. Paul's Episcopal Church and attended by more than two hundred adults each Sunday. He has indicated his scholarly ability in the authorship of two books, *Honest Prayer*, which was chosen the Seabury Book for Lent in 1973, and *This Hebrew Lord*, as well as the publication of numerous articles.

It was with the publication of the latter book that the paths of the rector and the rabbi crossed, an interaction of thought patterns which derived from the search for Christian roots on the part of the former and the inquisitive desire for clarification on the part of the latter. Mr. Spong's pilgrimage had caused him to raise serious questions about many of the traditional affirmations which were so easily verbalized but which had seemingly lost contact with their early Hebrew roots. Seeking to discover answers to basic questions with which he as a priest could live happily, he spent long hours in the study of the Jewish scriptures. Out of this quest there ultimately developed *This Hebrew Lord*. Rabbi Spiro, intrigued by this title, secured a copy of the volume for his personal reading, and eventually called Mr. Spong to suggest a public debate on the content of the book. He later expressed the idea that he read the book to determine how the Christian Christ would emerge out of the Jewish Yahveh, how "this Hebrew Lord" would arise out of the Jewish traditions. During his reading of the book this expectation was never satisfied.

The conversations between Mr. Spong and Rabbi Spiro were attended by an immediate attitude of mutual respect and a deep sharing of viewpoints considerably different from each other. So exciting was the exchange that it soon became apparent to both of them that the electric experience which they were sharing should lead to more than a single debate on a book. It also should examine a wide range of issues between Christians and Jews. Thus the idea of a Jewish-Christian dialogue was conceived, involving the congregations of St. Paul's and Beth Ahabah.

THE DIALOGUE: FORMAT AND REACTIONS

As arrangements for the dialogue were finalized, the rabbi and rector agreed to have four sessions seeking to clarify those issues which both unite and separate Judaism and Christianity, two at St. Paul's Episcopal Church and two at Congregation Beth Ahabah. All sessions were scheduled at regular worship hours for the respective congregations, with the idea that the two congregations would share in these worship experiences. Opportunity was also provided on all four occasions for the worship participants to enter into dialogue in a more informal setting with the rector and the rabbi following the services. In addition to these dialogic occasions, Mr. Spong introduced the series at St. Paul's with an address on the Jewish roots of Christianity, while Dr. Spiro concluded the series with an address at Beth Ahabah on the ways in which Christianity has served to further the cause of Judaism.

This dialogue was a distinct service to the Richmond community, for this was the first occasion where extensive dialogue had taken place between Jewish and Christian congregations. There had been numerous earlier occasions where types of communication had taken place, such as "Brotherhood Week" pulpit exchanges. These exchanges unfortunately tend to focus only on surface issues. This dialogue, however, gave the members of St. Paul's and Beth Ahabah an opportunity to confront their similarities and differences in a substantive way. Because of the considerable newspaper publicity which was given to the dialogue, similar opportunity was provided for the broader Richmond community.

It is difficult to assess the impact of the dialogue upon the two congregations primarily involved. Needless to say, there are always Jews and Christians who see no need for this type of exchange, whether this attitude develops out of carefully masked prejudices, out of a conviction that the current Jewish-Christian relationship is quite satisfactory, or out of a basic disinterest. The mood in both congregations, however, has been character- ized by inquisitiveness, expectation, openness, and sincerity. Both congregations attended the dialogue sessions in numbers which clearly reflected their interest.

Individuals who had never participated in any formalized study of Judaism sat on the edges of the pews as Rabbi Spiro responded to Mr. Spong's questions, seeking to clarify his understanding of Judaism. Jewish participants listened with equal interest and anticipation as Mr. Spong, answering Rabbi Spiro's questions, spelled out his understanding of Christianity. In the discussions following all four dialogue sessions, large numbers of the congregations remained to question either the rabbi or the rector. The questions were penetrating and honest; the responses returned with equal clarity and honesty.

Because of continuing interest in the dialogic approach to understanding divergent as well as similar beliefs and practices in the two religions, the rabbi and the rector developed a joint piece on Christmas-Hanukah as the festival season for both congregations approached. This presentation is found at the end of this volume. One of the clearest evaluations of the dialogue's effect is that conversations still are heard in both large and small groups within and beyond the two congregations.

When Rabbi Spiro made a passing comment that he and Mr. Spong were discussing the possibility of continuing the dialogue, there was an immediate positive response from members of both congregations. The reality of Jewish roots had for the first time become pivotal to the thought of many Christians, and the possibility of a meaningful and productive relationship with a sister faith had become real to many Jews. Twentieth-century individuals were suddenly swept back to those very issues which divided Jews and Christians during the first century of the Christian era. Was there the possibility that we might be able to deal more constructively now with the issues which historically made the relationship between Judaism and Christianity difficult? Whether or not that question was answered corporately or individually is less important than the emerging attitude which helped to create the question, for it was only as the Jewish and Christian communities began to confront each other with the proper questions that meaningful answers could develop.

Within the larger Richmond community, the reactions were quite varied. A number of individuals, not members either of St. Paul's or Beth Ahabah, came to the dialogue sessions and obviously found them to be productive. Rabbi Spiro and Mr. Spong were invited by the Richmond Clergy Association to present a program which would deal with the primary themes of their dialogue. Recordings of the sessions have been replayed on station WRVA in Richmond on four successive Sunday mornings. The Public Service Television affiliate (WCVE-TV) in Richmond requested Rabbi Spiro and Mr. Spong to repeat the dialogue with one hour of exchange between the rabbi and the rector and a second hour devoted to questions from the viewing public. This is sufficient to say that a significant number of individuals within the Richmond community found the dialogue exciting and challenging.

One cannot claim, however, that the reaction of the Richmond community was one of consensus and acceptance. A number of letters were published on the editorial page of the *Richmond Times-Dispatch*, some of which were extremely derogatory, while others either complimented the participants or defended their right to enter into the dialogue. For example, a Christian writer asserted that "there is a place in Christendom

for those of us who are not biblical and credal literalists."
Counterbalancing this openness was a letter stating that it had
been "interesting and most nauseating to read Mr. Spong's
statements denying the virgin birth and Rabbi Spiro's statements that God was a changing God and imperfect." [1] Very
little negative reaction came from the Jewish community, but
this should not imply community consent.

The Union of Orthodox Jewish Congregations of America
adopted a resolution in its 1966 Convention which stated that
"the Jewish people must reject . . . any endeavor to become
engaged in dialogues concerning our faith and its theological
foundations." This is still an operative statement and is echoed
in the *Joint Program Plan for Jewish Community Relations
1974–75* proposal that "Jewish participation in any council
arrangement that seeks to deal in matters of theology or
religious thought is to be avoided."

Clearly both the Jewish and Christian communities have their
dissident elements when the subject of interfaith dialogue is
mentioned. Some awareness of the interaction of Judaism and
Christianity through the centuries helps to clarify why certain
attitudes have developed, both among Jews and Christians.

JEW AND CHRISTIAN: SOME HISTORICAL
PERSPECTIVES

The reader will note that in Rabbi Spiro's concluding
response in the final dialogue held at St. Paul's Episcopal
Church he encouraged a concentration upon the present and
hope in the future rather than upon the failures of the past. I find
this attitude commendable, and yet it is imperative that the
Christian be aware of the realities of history in order that the
Jewish attitude be understandable.

The first four centuries of the Jewish-Christian relationship set
the tone for the interaction which would occur during the
Middle Ages, the era during which the Jewish-Christian relationship totally deteriorated. Available evidence indicates that
the earliest followers of Jesus were Jewish, and the first chapters

of the Acts of the Apostles depict a community very much a part of Jewish life and practice. As the followers of Jesus moved beyond Palestine into the Greco-Roman world, however, the Church appealed to Gentiles. One recognizes this particularly in the writings of Paul, who emphasized faith as the proper vehicle for affirming a relationship between God and man. This necessarily excluded certain ritual acts associated with Judaism, especially circumcision. Such an emphasis had the effect of drawing into the Church those Gentiles who had been favorably impressed with Jewish theology but were unwilling to embrace certain ritual practices.

As a majority of the early Christians were uncircumcised Gentiles, a significant problem was created for the zealous Jew who took seriously all of Judaism's ritual requirements. When circumcision was ignored, there were repercussions in the realm of social fellowship. The zealous Jew was convinced of the necessity for him to abide by the legal injunctions of Judaism, and contact with Gentiles caused difficulty in the practice of circumcision and the dietary laws. He was convinced that it was defiling for him to engage in significant interaction with the uncircumcised and to participate in table fellowship with those who ignored the dietary laws. From a Jewish perspective, therefore, the segregation of Jews and Christians was essential.

In this fashion the Jews gradually became a "problem" for the Christians, although it is clear that Paul did not view the situation this way. The Letter to the Romans (9–11) expressed his conviction that the refusal of Jews to accept Jesus was consonant with the purpose of God. When the Jews rejected that message, Paul then turned to the Gentiles with the expectation that eventually the Jews would hear and respond. It is equally clear that Paul's view, expressed around the middle of the first century, did not prevail. The relationship of Jews and Christians continually deteriorated, resulting finally in a separation so complete that it was even recognized by the Roman government at the end of the century. This brought about the loss of protective status that Christianity enjoyed as a branch of Judaism. Consequently, the bulk of the persecution experienced by the early Christians during the first two centuries of the Church's existence emanated from Rome rather than from Jewish authorities. I would not suggest that hostilities which derived from Jewish hands never corrupted the Jewish-Christian situation, but certainly the popular ideas about the radical persecution of the early Christians by the Jews are exaggerated.

Thus the Christian recognition of the Jewish "problem" derived from the failure of the Jews to respond favorably when the Church proclaimed Jesus of Nazareth to be messiah. Early Christians were convinced that what they saw so readily would be recognized by the Jews when the message was clearly and forcefully delivered. We must understand, however, that many of these early proclaimers, being Hellenistically oriented, did not have an experiential background in Judaism. They did not understand the problems which the Jew experienced in associating Jesus with the messiah. Jesus simply did not fulfill the expectations of most Jews. According to Judaism, the exaltation of a human figure to divine status was blatant heresy. Thus most of the Jews could respond positively neither to the Jesus of history proclaimed by the Church nor to the Christ of faith who was actually the object of worship within the context of the Church's existence. We recognize, moreover, that the Church was also a problem for Judaism, because it multiplied so rapidly. As is so often the lesson of history, the spoils go to the victor and the victor is that body which amasses the strongest base of power and authority!

The determining factor for the resolution of the Jewish-Christian problem was ultimately political. In the year 312 the Emperor Constantine embraced Christianity, although Christianity was not adopted as the official religion of the Roman Empire until a later date.[2] Nonetheless, when the emperor embraced Christianity, the seeds were planted for the growth of a bitter conflict between Christians and Jews.

In 313 Constantine issued the Edict of Milan, which assured toleration for Christians throughout the empire.[3] It is unfortunate that the Christians, having now gained recognition and toleration, did not recall their several centuries of persecution.

The Church throughout this period was attempting to formulate a type of orthodox affirmation to assure unity and to establish its own position by formulating credal statements which set it apart more distinctly from Judaism. One of the clearest examples of this is the Nicene Creed, which emanated from the Council of Nicaea, convened in 325. Admittedly the Council must be seen primarily against the controversy which swirled around Arius in Egypt. It had repercussions not only for Arius and his followers, however, who became heretics via the credal statement, but also for the Jews who had found in the fourth century some haven in Egypt because of the Arian viewpoint. The impact of the stance assumed by the Church became apparent in a decree issued in 329 which forbade Jews to hold Christian slaves or to convert the pagan, the latter being punishable by death.

One other fourth-century example depicts the situation of the Jews during the period, namely the preaching of Ambrose John Chrysostom, whose oratory earned him the name "the golden-mouthed." Chrysostom was much concerned with converting all pagans to Christianity. The Jews were the "pagans" who received his deepest scorn. In one sermon he went so far as to assert: "The Jews are possessed by demons, they are handed over to impure spirits." [4] This quotation is sufficient to indicate the reaction arising in significant Christian quarters. Most Christians had forgotten that Judaism was their heritage and that Jesus himself was a Jew.

During the papacy of Gregory the Great (590–604), the style of Jewish-Christian relations for the Middle Ages was set. Cecil Roth, an eminent Jewish historian writing about the period, stated:

> Positive persecution was indeed discouraged and forced baptism deprecated. The Jews might enjoy liberty of worship and maintain their synagogues, though they were allowed neither to erect new ones nor to embellish the old. On the other hand, they were not to be encouraged to fresh "insolence." Proselytism on their part was to be sternly repressed. The imitation of Jewish rites by Christians was

prohibited. Their ownership of Christian slaves was not to be tolerated under any condition. Even the employment of Jewish physicians, who might obtain physical and, ultimately, moral control over their patients was not to be allowed, and secular rulers were sternly warned against appointing any Jewish officials, in however unimportant a capacity.[5]

In this quotation, reference is made to forced baptisms. The idea developed that it was in the interest of the Jew to be baptized, even by force, thus assuring the salvation of his soul. This practice was especially prevalent with Jewish children. Eventually it was determined that such children should not be permitted to remain within the corrupting influence of Judaism. The Fourth Council of Toledo in 633 even gave official sanction to wresting these baptized children from their parents. The deterioration continued as the Ninth Council of Toledo in 655 decreed that the baptized Jew must always remain in the presence of a Christian clergyman during any Jewish or Christian holy season so there would be no relapse into Jewish practices at these times.

Early in the Middle Ages the Jew was excluded from many professions; the military; and, in most instances, from government service, a notable exception to the latter being certain periods in Spain. During the medieval period, however, his restrictions were much greater. As the feudal system developed, the Jews were excluded from the land because the feudal system was a Christian structure. As the Jews migrated to the cities, they found the various craft guilds dominated also by Christians. Once again the Jews were ostracized. Frequently the Jews found the area of finance to be the major avenue open to them. This was not a vocational pursuit they chose, but one into which they were forced in order to survive.

The loss of status and power for Jews in the medieval period was so great that they had to seek alliances simply to live. They sought a direct relationship to the crown in order to mitigate oppressive taxation. By the ninth century, Jews had become the property of the crown in various countries.[6] The detrimental effects of the taxation which would come from the crown were not envisioned. Jews soon found themselves financing a significant portion of the king's projects.

One negative aspect of this relationship was seen in the period of the Crusades. Islam, which emerged as a faith structure in the seventh century, was by this time a powerful political and military force in the medieval world. News drifted westward that Muslims were desecrating Christian shrines in Palestine, particularly in Jerusalem. This precipitated a sermon by Pope Urban II before the Council of Clermont on November 26, 1095, which encouraged Christians to take whatever steps were necessary to recover the Holy Land and its shrines from the infidel. In financing the eight crusades, from 1096 until 1291, much of the revenue was derived from the Jews. This ignoble situation was particularly difficult since many of the crusaders never reached Jerusalem, but instead vented their religious wrath upon the infidels who were nearer at hand, namely the Jews. Countless numbers of Jews lost their lives because of crusader zeal.

Fact and interpretation became totally confused during this period. Anyone having any awareness of Judaism knew of the Jewish ritual restrictions regarding the blood of a slain animal, a dietary restriction which the Jews traced to the Noachian covenant (Gen. 9:1-7). In spite of this, rumors spread and were accepted as fact that the Jews ritually slaughtered Christian children and used their blood for the making of Passover matzah. Numerous instances of Jewish persecution are traceable to this interpretation of a Christian child found dead, whatever the cause.[7] This ignorance, fanned by the fires of prejudice, ignited into unimaginable brutality.

The councils of the Church continued to manifest considerable anti-Semitism, exemplified by the Third Lateran Council of 1179 which decreed that Christians could not live among Jews. While the ghetto did not officially arise for approximately three and a half centuries, this was the beginning of ghetto life for the Jews. The restriction was positively stated in that it was the Christian who was prohibited from living among the infidels, but the end result was the same. It was the Jew who was segregated in quarters where he would not contaminate the Christian.

The Fourth Lateran Council of 1215 carried anti-Semitism one step further. At all times the Jew must wear a distinguishing badge. This was an attempt to identify the Jew so that Christians might refrain from doing business with him, and various types of social contact or religious interaction might be avoided. The Jew was gradually but assuredly being pushed into subcitizenship.

The spirit of the times was characterized by an edict of Pope Gregory IX, when in 1242 he encouraged raids on Jewish synagogues for the purpose of gathering Hebrew manuscripts. The result was the burning of twenty-four cartloads of manuscripts in the streets of Paris.

Christians were convinced of the superiority of their faith structure and of their subsequent responsibility to bring the gospel message to the Jew. I have already commented on the enforced baptisms which took place with some frequency, but another indicator is found in the decree of Pope Nicholas III in 1278 when Christians were given the freedom of Jewish pulpits. By this action the Christian had the prerogative of entering the synagogue at any occasion of Jewish worship, assuming the pulpit, and preaching for the conversion of the Jews. It was demanded of the Jews that they remain seated as the Christian spokesman made his proclamation. Quite obviously, one could not legislate that the Jews listen.

The predicament of the Jews was horrible throughout this era. They no longer felt any freedom to move about at will to seek a place where freer expression might be found. They recognized the fact that the crusaders who came upon them on the open roads would view them as the infidel enemy, and thus there was nothing to do but remain where they were and try to survive. There was no season of the year when the Jews experienced greater fear and actual physical agony than the Easter season. During the Passiontide, Christians sensed themselves under particular obligation to rectify the wrong they judged to have been committed against Jesus by the Jews. Pogrom followed pogrom during this period of the year, and the slightest provocation was seized upon as sufficient rationale for further persecutions.

Eventually the Jews found themselves stripped of possessions and power. Any reason for maintaining the Jews in an area was thereby removed, and thus the final ignominy occurred. In 1290, King Edward I of England issued a decree demanding that all Jews leave the country within three months. As a result, the westward movement of the Jews during the prior millennium was reversed and an eastward trek initiated.[8] This manner of dealing with the Jews was not limited to England, for in France Philip the Fair issued a similar decree in 1306 which gave the Jews only one month to prepare for their departure, with all of their properties being confiscated by the crown. The most devastating blow was to come in 1492 when Queen Isabella and King Ferdinand issued a decree demanding the expulsion of all Jews from Spain.

It was in Spain that cultural creativity among Jews reached its height. Jewish men of letters, medicine, science, and government were influential throughout the realm. This explains why in Spain a phenomenon occurred, which in terms of its extensiveness is unparalleled in Jewish history, namely the massive "conversion" of Jews to Christianity in order to maintain their position. Even in its early stages, the inquisition, which began in 1480, was in large measure aimed at these individuals.

The situation was no better for the Jews of Italy. On Rosh Hashanah in 1553, by papal decree, all known copies of the Talmud were burned in Rome. The Jews were obviously moving toward another period of intense persecution, which ultimately climaxed in 1555 with a papal bull reinstituting all of the medieval legislation for Jews living in Italy. Earlier, in 1516, the Jews in Venice had been restricted to a separate quarter known as Ghetto Nuovo, or "New Foundry." Walled enclosures were established in Italy, and this phenomenon spread rapidly throughout Europe.

The ghetto proved to be a radical test for the Jews physically, emotionally, and religiously.[9] For more than two centuries, the main thrust of Jewish life was restricted behind walls where

Christian gatekeepers governed entrance and exit. Physically, the Jews who emerged from the ghetto were several inches shorter than the Jews who entered and were stooped in posture. Emotionally, an intense hatred for all Gentiles was engendered, while an uncommon allegiance to fellow Jews was encouraged. Religiously, the love of learning could hardly be propagated under such conditions; and thus the general level of Hebrew scholarship deteriorated considerably during this period.

As Roland de Corneille suggests, it would be very easy to lay this treatment at the doorsteps of superstition and barbarism during the medieval period; but the fact is that much of this persecution occurred during the Renaissance. He states very clearly:

> . . . while history will not allow us to lay the blame upon the doorstep of medievalism, it also refuses to permit us the scapegoat of the papacy or the Roman Catholic Church. The temptation to lay the responsibility there is made all the more attractive by the fact that the plight of the Jews was gradually ameliorated during the centuries which followed the Protestant Reformation. Therefore, it has occurred to some people that Protestantism provided a kind of driving force towards the establishment of tolerance and more humane attitudes towards Jews. As a matter of historical fact, however, Protestantism did nothing of the kind . . . nothing positive emerged from it to change the persistent negative stereotypes by which the Christian habitually judged them. Any opportunity which Protestantism had to rectify the past, or at least to establish a segment of the Church on a new footing, was lost.[10]

As a precipitator of what would later be designated the Protestant Reformation, Martin Luther nailed his ninety-five theses to the door of the castle church of Wittenberg in 1517. Luther was at this point sympathetic to the plight of the Jews, and he was convinced that the Jews would respond favorably when they heard his proclamation of the gospel. His Jewish audiences, however, did not find his proclamation of the New Testament to be any more appealing than what had been proclaimed earlier. The result was that Luther became exceedingly anti-Semitic, his sermons clearly demonstrating this changed attitude.[11] Unfortunately, one cannot point to anything concrete which either Luther or John Calvin did to help alleviate the situation of the Jews as it had developed during the Middle Ages. The inhumane treatment of the Jews characteristic of the Church during this period was not abated by Protestantism. Roland de Corneille summarizes well the situation when he states:

> So far as the relationship of the Church to the Jewish people is concerned, there are few exceptions to the rule that at no time did Christianity champion the cause of the Jews. It was only when movements outside the Church such as Humanism, Capitalism and Nationalism, brought their influence to bear that the situation improved at all.[12]

De Corneille's statement makes clear that the Church has more often been the culprit in the Jews' difficulties than their benefactor. One can refer to the ideologies of humanism, capitalism, and nationalism as sources of deliverance for Jews, because people caught up in these movements have delivered Jews from their oppressors. The clearest example of this is in the French Revolution of 1789. With its emphases on dignity and equality, it was impossible for the Jew to remain ostracized within the ghetto. Napoleon's soldiers razed the walls and gates of the ghettos, and once again the Jew was free to assume his rightful place in society. Gradually throughout Europe the ghetto walls crumbled.

The responsibility of the Church for the treatment of the Jews during World War II will be debated for many years to come. One-third of the world's Jewish population was destroyed in Hitler's gas chambers and furnaces.

The extent of the Church's culpability is questionable. One

must acknowledge, however, that anti-Semitism, which existed historically in the Christian Church, had provided a foundation upon which Hitler could build successfully. It is a fact that few Church leaders spoke out in defense of the Jews. The voice of the Church throughout the world was basically silent.

SOME VIEWS REGARDING DIALOGUE

We must live with the facts, however, and seek to rectify those wrongs which punctuate history. We must speak to the sins of the fathers, recognizing that the sins of the fathers are visited upon the children. So long as prejudice continues, it is necessary for all men to seek new understandings which will oppose that prejudice. A new understanding has been realized at St. Paul's Episcopal Church and Congregation Beth Ahabah through dialogue.

Various types of communication have taken place since the emergence of the Church, but it is doubtful that the word *dialogue* accurately describes these forms of interaction. Rabbi Jakob J. Petuchowski defines dialogue as follows:

> . . . talk among equals, born of mutual respect, and with full awareness of where the division lies, dedicated to the furtherance of a shared concern.[13]

Accepting this definition, disputations, apologetics, and polemics—but not dialogue—have been characteristic of the Jewish-Christian relationship.

Rabbi Petuchowski makes clear that one should not judge the Christian as being uniquely interested in establishing his own faith. While traditionally Christendom has envisioned the ultimate coming of the Jew to a Christian affirmation, so too has Judaism anticipated that during the age of the messiah all men would turn to God and accept the Jewish understanding of Torah.[14]

It is at this juncture that the real starting point for dialogue must be found. However, the thought develops,[15] one must reach the point in either community where the integrity and validity of the other's faith pursuit is acknowledged. This acknowledgment excludes any attempt, however, subtle, to proselytize. To approach the dialogue with a perspective other than this is to express a basic contempt for the faith affirmation of the dialogic partner.

Dialogue must clearly define the intention of the dialogue situation, express the grandeur and beauty of each tradition, and clarify the issues which bind and separate Jews and Christians. We can hardly expect a dialogue to be successful when there is uncertainty and ambiguity on the part of the participants. We frequently fail in our efforts because such clarification is not a part of the foundation work for the actual dialogue.

Since the Bible is pivotal in both Judaism and Christianity, it assumes an indispensable role in dialogue. In the Hebrew Bible there are passages which refer to the dominance of the Jews over other nations as well as those which set forth Israel's revelatory mission to all peoples. Similarly, in Christian scriptures there is much that may be interpreted in terms of Christianity's relationship to all men; but it is clear that a large portion of the New Testament was written in a polemical atmosphere against the Jews who were seen as the primary deterrent to the fulfillment of Christian expectations. No constructive end is served by the excision of such passages which both the Jew and the Christian find offensive.

As a beginning point Jews and Christians can meet in an open and constructive study of the scriptures. They must look together at variant interpretations of problematic passages and try to understand why there are differences. Objectivity must be sought and prejudices recognized in order that honesty might prevail.

The point must be reached, moreover, where another's humanity is primary, whether Jew or Christian, male or female, black or white. To use Martin Buber's expression, every meeting of Jew and Christian should be an "I-Thou" relationship.

It is this goal of fully personal relationships toward which we strive. Participants in the Jewish-Christian dialogue at St. Paul's

Episcopal Church and Congregation Beth Ahabah do not claim to have achieved that elusive goal, but significant strides have been made in that direction. A rector and a rabbi have developed a relationship of mutual acceptance and respect. Members of the two congregations have engaged each other in significant communication. Had these two dividends constituted the total return, the dialogue still would have been worthwhile. The fact is that many individuals have become fuller human beings as a result of this dialogue. The reverberations of the dialogue will continue to resound for many years at St. Paul's Episcopal Church, at Congregation Beth Ahabah, and hopefully in the larger Richmond community.

NOTES

1. Letters dated Nov. 22 and 6, 1974, respectively.
2. See Kenneth Scott Latourette, *A History of Christianity* (Harper & Brothers, 1953), pp. 91–93.
3. Ibid., p. 92.
4. Quotation found in Roland de Corneille, *Christians and Jews* (Harper & Row, Publishers, 1966), pp. 20–21. See also Gregory Baum, *The Jews and the Gospel* (The Newman Press, 1961), p. 6.
5. Cecil Roth, *A History of the Jews*, rev. ed. (Schocken Books, 1970), p. 145.
6. de Corneille, p. 24. See also Roth, pp. 195–197, who treats the impact of this aspect of the social revolution experienced by the Jews.
7. Roth, pp. 183–185, discusses this phenomenon. Bernard Malamud, in *The Fixer* (Dell Publishing Co., Inc., 1966), used this motif in the context of Czarist Russia to portray the story of Yakov Bok.
8. Ibid., pp. 208–209; Roth suggests that more than 16,000 Jews were displaced as a result of this decree.
9. Ibid., pp. 273 ff.; Roth has an excellent chapter on Jewish life in the ghetto.
10. de Corneille, pp. 34–35.
11. Ibid., pp. 36–37, quotes the beginning of one of Luther's sermons, the first sentence of which is as follows: "What then shall we Christians do with this damned rejected race of Jews? . . ."
12. Ibid., p. 39.

13. Jakob J. Petuchowski, "The Jewish-Christian Dialogue," *The Jewish Spectator* (March–April, 1965), p. 8.
14. Ibid., p. 12.
15. Ibid., pp. 13–14.

chapter I

JEWISH GIFTS TO CHRISTIANITY

The dialogue began in the church as Christians sought to acknowledge and embrace their debt to the Jews.

Christians and Jews are both the children of Abraham. We spring from the same soil; we possess the same roots; we rise from the same heritage. This dialogue between Christians and Jews is designed to explore that common background in depth; to seek our areas of deep agreement and compatibility; to clarify and lay bare those points where we are destined to be eternally in conflict, where our very identity demands that we stand over against one another.

We Christians enter this experience because we believe that we must be able to hear and respond to a presentation of faith and a view of life that is specifically different from our own. Secondly, by this dialogue, we hope to confront our distinctiveness as Christians. There is an irreducible essence of the Christian revelation which is distinct from the packaging in which it is traditionally presented. Thirdly, it is our desire to expose continually the latent anti-Semitism that lurks in the dark crevices of Western civilization. Too often have we Christians been marked by an unlovely and unloving arrogance in our relationship to the other great worship traditions of our world—an arrogance that hardly brings honor to those who claim to be followers of Jesus of Nazareth.

This dialogue must begin by sensitizing Christians to our ancient Jewish roots. We must learn to bow deeply and humbly toward the Judaism of Moses and the prophets with a reverence born of a genuine and acknowledged debt. For this Judaism is the parent of Christianity.

From the extraordinary concept of one God, originally perceived by the Jews in the thirteenth century B.C., has sprung all that is Judaism and all that is Christianity. From the perception of one God—the same God—Judaism and Christianity continue to evolve throughout all of history.

As the origin of the Christian revelation, Judaism is the tradition from which came the Christian Lord, Jesus of Nazareth. Judaism was his ancestry and Judaism gave him birth. Judaism nurtured him, instructed him, shaped and formed him. Judaism was his heritage, his family, his home, his school, his neighborhood, his worship tradition, his world. He read and he memorized Jewish scripture, our Old Testament. He applied the principles of Moses to his daily life. He prayed to the God Yahveh, and to that God he gave his intimate new Aramaic name, *Abba,* which means "dear Father."[1] He sang, for his hymns of praise, the psalms of the scriptures. Jesus was in every respect a descendant and an heir of Abraham, Moses, and David.

Judaism produced our Lord, and it is from Judaism that we Christians have received him. As all the world knows, it is because of Judaism that Christianity has its being.

During World War II when anti-Semitism was rife in Nazi Germany, the Axis ally to the south in Italy, Benito Mussolini, began to make similar anti-Semitic noises. Pope Pius XII spoke on national radio to warn the leaders of the state that every Christian considered himself or herself a spiritual Jew and that anti-Semitism would not be tolerated by the Catholic Church in Italy. Mussolini never again tried to heat up those passions.

The Pope was right. We Christians are to our deepest cores spiritual Jews, whether we know it or not, whether we acknowledge it or not. Not only did Judaism give us our Lord, but also out of the Old Testament, the Hebrew tradition, we have received our understanding of God the Father, creator of heaven and earth.

There is a popular cliché among unthinking Christians which

asserts that the Old Testament gives us the God of justice and the New Testament gives us the God of love. That is simply not so! The God of Judaism and the God of Christianity is one consistent God, combining love with justice on every page of the Bible. Nowhere is the love of God more powerfully illustrated than in Israel's deliverance from slavery in Egypt or Israel's elevation as the chosen people, told us in the Book of Exodus. Even the heart of the moral code of Judaism, the Ten Commandments, is given not simply as a law or a duty; it is, rather, the human response of love to God's initiating love. Because Yahveh, their God, has brought them out of Egypt, they are called to respond in love by having no other gods, making no graven images, and keeping his name and his day holy. Because the love of their God is seen breaking them out of bondage and slavery—and whatever else distorts their human spirit—they are called in response to deal lovingly with one another by honoring their parents and by refraining from murder, adultery, stealing, lying, and coveting; indeed, by loving one another as God has loved them. It is the God of love who is seen by the prophet Hosea in the eighth century B.C. He tells us very powerfully and very dramatically of this God who loves Israel, even when Israel is unfaithful, in the same manner that Hosea has loved his wife, Gomer, even when she was unfaithful to him. The God of love is writ large in the Hebrew tradition.

The Hebrew people saw this God of love as the author of creation, and this produced among them their wondrous attitude toward life and the world. In their story of the creation, God's life-giving spirit was pictured as brooding over the waters of chaos in order to bring it to life and order and being, almost as a setting hen might brood over her nest. That which God created, in all of the magnificent physical, material detail, the Hebrew people knew was good; and for the Jew this meant the world never could be an evil place. It never could be a place to be avoided or from which to retreat. "This is my Father's world," they asserted, and they knew the world was endowed with the holiness of God. So to meet their creator God, they dared to enter as deeply as possible into the stream of life.

Never did the Jew isolate God in some ghetto called "religion." Indeed, there is no Hebrew word in that whole vocabulary that we can translate accurately with our word *religion.* God, for the Jew, was not the God of religion; he was the God of life. He permeated all of existence. No place was outside his purpose. He revealed himself in the living moments of history. The Jewish God was not a memory isolated in the dim and distant past; he was, rather, a power and a force that stood ever before his people, calling them to enter into the future—to live and to be and to walk into the unknown, for tomorrow held no fear for those who believed that God was ready to be met, ready to be engaged in the throbbing, pulsing events of life.

Out of this idea there came the Jewish sense of worship. Worship was a call to enter life, a call to meet God, a call to love one another, a call to be all that life was created to be. Worship was not a pious activity cut off from the rest of one's existence. If God was the source of life, as they believed him to be, then anything that distorted life had to be contrary to God's will. Worship for the Hebrew could never be separated from human justice, and eventually this knowledge enabled the Hebrew people to produce the great leaders who were not duplicated in the life of any other ancient folk. These leaders were called prophets. Their insights seared the flesh of human unrighteousness, and they stamped indelibly on this Jewish people—and, through Judaism, on us Christians—the perception that the worship of God was human justice being offered heavenward, and that human justice was the divine worship of God being lived out among men. Anything other than that was, to the Jew, idolatry.

These prophets have become special heroes to me in the course of my life. They are like living, flesh-and-blood friends. To study Israel's history is to watch them emerge time after time on the world's stage; and when they leave it, the world is never the same.

There was Amos, the sheepherder, the tender of the sycamore trees, compelled to go to Bethel to witness to the God of justice.

There was Hosea, the quiet and dignified man who saw, symbolically, in his own domestic tragedy, the relationship between God and Israel. There was Isaiah, the diplomat, the unofficial advisor to kings, the Bernard Baruch of ancient Israel, who saw the hand of God in every moving event of life. There was Micah, the country lawyer, who yearned above all things to practice before the supreme court of the universe. There was Jeremiah, the sensitive soul, whose ability to weep characterized Judah at the moment of its destruction. There was Ezekiel, the prophet-priest, who walked that death march into Babylon and kept alive the torch of Judaism in captivity. Finally, there was that unknown prophet we call Second Isaiah, who described a way of salvation that I am convinced Jesus of Nazareth deliberately sought to live out. Indeed, I do not think it is possible for any Christian to understand his Lord unless he sees him in the light of Second Isaiah's portrait of the servant figure.

Jesus our Christ was in the great Jewish tradition of prophecy, and we cannot understand him outside that tradition. When Jesus was asked to summarize the Jewish law, he responded in a typically Jewish way: "You must bring together your love of God and your love of your neighbor, for on this all else hangs." When he told the parable of the judgment, the test of whether one loved God or believed in God was not intellectual assent to creeds or regular participation in "churchy" activities. His questions were, rather, "Did you feed the hungry? Did you give water to the thirsty or clothe the naked or visit the sick and imprisoned? For if you did these things to the least person in human society, you have done them to God himself." Worship and justice were merged in our Hebrew Lord.

For Judaism and for the Hebrew Jesus of Nazareth, the act of worship could never descend into a pious, sentimental irrelevance, because the God they served was the source of life and the source of love and the ground of being. The Jews saw the wonder and beauty of life; and they taught the world to worship the creator God by loving his creation in all of its forms: inanimate, animate, and human.

Hebrew thought is not monolithic either theologically or

historically, so when we dip into this faith of our fathers we can come up with different and even competing ideas, all of which can be presented as Jewish. Different eras seemed to emphasize different truths. Pre-exilic Hebrew thought was in many ways quite different from post-exilic thought.

I think this is best seen when we seek to embrace the Hebrew attitude toward life's darker shadows, the distortions of creation, the inhumanity in human life. This people, especially in the Yahvist tradition of the pre-exilic southern kingdom, saw the destructive power of evil that thwarted God's purpose. They were aware of warped people and insecure hearts and unloving lives; and they called this darkness "sin," a word that for the ancient Jew described the being of human life out of which evil deeds inevitably arise. Evil to them was the misuse of creation out of one's inner need for love or for power. Evil was the spread of death where life was God's intention. Evil was the threat of hate in a world where love and freedom that brought fullness were desired. Sin was seen in the human inability to accept the limitation of our humanity. It was seen in our jealousy and envy, in our status seeking, and in our prejudice. No people were ever more realistic about human nature than the Jews, and this insight was given to the world in the myth of the fall in the Garden of Eden. At the same time no people more positively asserted that this broken, fallen humanity, this distorted world, was not what God intended when he created us. So in Judaism we see a refusal to lower the vision, a refusal to identify what is with what should be or what shall be.

Finally, the Jewish people were always a nation of dreamers; and their dreams they personified, producing the hope that messiah would come. Messiah's purpose to the Hebrew mind was to call humanity back to its meaning in creation. Messiah was to bring into life and into human history the power of the love of God which restores us to what God intended us to be, thus creating peace by ending our inner alienation.

Judaism has transmitted this rich heritage to Christian people. It has given us our Lord Jesus Christ, the meaning of God the Father as the source of love and the author of creation. It has given us an attitude of reverence and joy toward life in God's world. It has bound together, in an inseparable way for us, divine worship and human justice. It has looked at human life with a realism that understands sin, and it has given birth to an eternal hope that fulfillment is possible in human history.

We are in debt to Judaism for our very life. Christians could not be Christians had not Jews been faithful to Judaism. Yet today Christian and Jew stand deeply divided. The issue which divides us is the same issue which created Christian people. It is the revelation of God in a Hebrew life, Jesus of Nazareth. This is a division which we cannot remove and which we cannot ignore. We can, however, listen to one another across that division. We can appreciate the power of each other's tradition. We can be sensitive to the insights that each gives to the world. We can love one another apart from the judgment of superiority and inferiority. And, for us Christians, we can discover anew in that process our own Christian uniqueness, gratefully received from a great worship tradition.

These are our goals in this Jewish-Christian dialogue.

NOTE

1. See Joachim Jeremias, *The Lord's Prayer* (Fortress Press, 1964).

chapter II

ON ONE FOOT: JUDAISM

The dialogue sought to let Christians hear from a rabbi about the basic nature of Judaism.

MR. SPONG: To begin this session of our dialogue, Rabbi Spiro, let me ask you the most basic and relevant question: What is Judaism?

RABBI SPIRO: To answer that question, I will relate an incident in my own tradition and history, for the same question was asked by a non-Jew of the famous Jew, Hillel, some two thousand years ago, or approximately thirty years before the birth of Jesus. The non-Jew asked Hillel to define Judaism while standing on one foot. Hillel was not the most agile person in the world, and so his answer had to be a brief distillation of what was already, by his time, two or three thousand years of Jewish tradition. In reply to the question, What is Judaism? Hillel said to the non-Jew, "That which is hateful to you do not do unto your fellow man. The rest is commentary; now go forth and learn." I know that statement is somewhat familiar to you, because it sounds like the one made by Jesus in the New Testament: "Do unto others what you would have them do unto you." Hillel formed it in the negative for good psychological reasons, because we can be more certain of what might harm another person than we can definitely know what might be of benefit to him. Most commandments of the Torah, for an important example, are in the negative because it is practicable to put the brakes on ourselves, to construct a behavioral framework in which to operate, to recognize our boundaries.

Hillel's response, therefore, to the pagan is, in my opinion, the essence of Judaism. Notice that Hillel, who was a teacher, added something very important to the statement by saying: "The rest is commentary; now go forth and learn." The going forth to learn—the details, all the ramifications, and how to fulfill them—is indispensable in the entire gamut of Jewish tradition.

I think another way of getting to the essence of Judaism is to go to the origins of Judaism. When we return to the source of something, we find there the keystone of its nature. Judaism, as a religion and as a people, originated at Mount Sinai where God concluded a covenant with the Israelites. That covenant was indeed a treaty or contract; this idea of God's making a contract with human beings constitutes the formative and decisive principle in the development of Judaism, preparing the way for everything to come. In principle it proclaimed: God enters into a contract with man. Therefore, God is not an absolute ruler, for an absolute ruler does not need a contract or a treaty or a constitution. The constitution is, in a sense, God's own being, his own power expressing itself, revealing itself to man. In entering into a contract with man, God binds himself to the conditions of the treaty as does man.

The conditions of the contract are spiritual and ethical. This indicates that in Judaism even God is bound to the moral commandments, to the ethical mandates of life. God relinquishes some of his own power in his revelation to man at Sinai in order for man to acquire that which makes him human, which is man's freedom: his freedom to make decisions, his freedom to select what is or is not of value. God has always known what is of value. The Ten Commandments are of value as are also many other commandments that we have in the Hebrew Bible (Old Testament), the New Testament, and in our religious traditions. However, God says to us that the supreme value—more important than any commandment—is not even stated explicitly: You shall be free! There is nothing more important than this freedom in order for the human being to be human. This is the quintessence of our entire Jewish tradition: that we have the value of freedom. "I have put before you life and death, blessing and curse. Choose life . . ." (Deut. 30:19). God gives us the power to choose, and in so doing he sacrifices some of his own power so that we can be truly human.

The capacity of freedom relates to another important concept of Judaism. Having the power to choose between good and evil or life and death means that we must be engaged not just in a life of belief, a life of mouthing ideas and ideology. We must also be committed to a life of action, of deed, of getting involved in our world and putting our ideas and values into action.

This, then, gives strength to the idea that Judaism is essentially a religious community which combines creed and deed. The two are indispensable, identified in their totality as a structure of values by which to live. They cannot be values unless those values are lived.

MR. SPONG: The beginning of Judaism, then, is really in the Exodus story, because it demonstrates this sense of freedom.

In order to understand the personal context out of which you speak, I wonder if you would tell us how you became a rabbi.

RABBI SPIRO: Initially, I became a rabbi for two reasons. First, I love Judaism, and secondly, I love teaching. When the two are combined, one has, essentially, a rabbi. I say this because a rabbi is a teacher of Judaism. As you know from New Testament statements and allusions, *rabbi,* the Hebrew word itself, means "my teacher." Rabbi is an affectionate word, because in Judaism there is something affectionate, warm, and beautiful about the teaching-learning process and the relationship between teacher and learner. Out of rabbinic literature comes this beautiful statement: "Teachers and students are society's most beautiful ornaments." Since I was ordained, it has been my goal to carry out in principle and in practice both my love of Judaism and the act and art of teaching Judaism.

Leading from this personal reflection, two major categories of Jewish values play a part in the decision to become a rabbi in addition to the definition of rabbi in Jewish tradition. These are the values of *knowledge* and *morality.* My task as a teacher is to provide knowledge, but not only knowledge as an end in itself. In Judaism, knowledge itself is a theological concept, a process of discovering that which is real and true. Knowledge is a pathway to God. If we trace the literature of Judaism through at least the past two thousand years, we find that knowledge appears to be even more important than prayer.

Prayer is, indeed, one pathway to God. In and beyond the synagogue, there are many types of liturgical expression; basically, however, study, learning, and knowledge are even more important than prayer. *Synagogue* is a Greek word which means "gathering place." But in Hebrew, one of the terms for synagogue, *bet midrash,* means "house of study." Yiddish-speaking Jews called the synagogue a *schul,* which means "school." The value of knowledge is based on the biblical commandment, *v'yadata,* which in Hebrew means "you shall know."

In the entire vocabulary of the very rich Hebrew language there is no word for *religion.* The nearest one can come to the word religion is another biblical phrase, *da-at Elohim,* meaning "knowledge of God." That is to say, one can know God, understand him in a limited way, and do his will by constantly engaging in the process of enlightening oneself through study. However, it is important to remember that knowledge is not an end in itself.

I will demonstrate this with an account from rabbinic literature. A debate took place between two rabbis on the question: Which is more important, learning or doing (ethical deeds)? One rabbi said learning is more important; the other rabbi said moral deeds are more important. A third rabbi offered a compromise, which was finally accepted: Study is more important but only when it leads to good deeds, because knowledge is then the foundation of wise decisions and wise actions.

One of the most dangerous persons in the world is the insensitive moralist or the "do-gooder" or, as the rabbi put it centuries ago, "the ass laden with books." We need knowledge in order to make wise decisions which lead to the performance of righteous deeds.

This is the essence of what it means to be a rabbi. A rabbi is supposed to be an ideal Jew.

MR. SPONG: In the debate between learning and doing, we might also add the category of *being* for later consideration.[1]

The point of issue between Christians and Jews is obviously the figure of Jesus, whom we Christians call "Christ." Why do you, as a Jew, and why does Judaism, find Jesus so unacceptable?

RABBI SPIRO: Yes, it is the crucial issue. I wish it were not, but only in the sense that if it were not an issue I think we could come together more closely. Yet, it will remain, and so we should think of ways of coming together in spite of it.

Let me answer the "unacceptability" part of your question. In the days of Jesus, as you know from your study of the history of the period, there was a great sense of immediacy and urgency, for it was a time of terrible persecution or, to quote Arnold Toynbee, "a time of trouble," when the Romans were oppressing every people in the Middle East. We read in the Book of Mark: "Jesus came into Galilee, spreading the gospel of the kingdom of God and saying that the time is fulfilled and the kingdom of God is at hand" (1:14). Here we have that sense of immediacy. The Jews of the period—and Jesus was a Jew—shared this feeling, because in this time of oppression, conditions were only growing worse. It was, according to the Jews, the time of the expected fulfillment of Isaiah's prophecy in chapter 11: "There shall come forth a shoot out of the stock of Jesse, and a twig shall grow forth out of his roots, and the spirit of the Lord shall rest upon him, the spirit of wisdom and understanding, the spirit of counsel and might, the spirit of knowledge, and the fear of the Lord." Jews were looking forward to one upon whom this prophecy would rest. One can envision the classic portrait of the messiah from Isaiah's writings. But the crucial question is: What was supposed to follow from this person upon whom the spirit rested? Historically, the effects should have been peace, harmony, enlightenment, and justice. In Jesus' time, the fulfillment of the coming of the messiah was absent. Jesus did not fulfill the expectation of the Jews, nor did the fulfillment follow his death.

There were others at this period who claimed to be the messiah, among these Theudas and Judas. Because of several would-be messiahs trying to inaugurate peace on earth and goodwill toward man during the Roman persecutions, Jews were becoming wary of personal messiahs as they saw the prophetic promises of Isaiah and other prophets were not being realized. This is probably the most important idea behind the unacceptability of Jesus. Eventually the concept of messianism was transformed, as skepticism grew concerning a personal messiah's power to achieve peace and justice in a world where there was no sense of goodwill. While the rabbis of the talmudic period (approximately first century through fifth century A.D.) still expressed a belief in the coming of a messiah, they also espoused the idea of the advent of messianic times. In other words, Jewish tradition began to stress the messianic ethic as a challenge to man to bring about messianic times and conditions along with a belief in the miraculous, supernatural advent of a messiah who would bring about an era of peace and justice.

There is ample evidence in Jewish literature of human responsibility and the messianic ethic. One example is a statement made by Rabbi Yochanan ben Zakkai, who lived some forty years later than Jesus, at the time that the temple in Jerusalem was destroyed. He wrote: "If you hold a seedling in your hand, and you hear the people shout, 'The messiah has come,' you must plant the seedling first, and then go out and welcome the messiah." This statement indicates the responsibility that man has to plant and grow, to bring peace and justice to the world.

In the Talmud there is a series of statements that the messiah will not come "until all qualities will be equal in men . . . until all evil judges cease out of Israel . . . until all money will be gone from the purse of man. . . ." While this passage expresses a belief in the messiah, the idea is subtly put forth that the messiah will not come until a messianic era of equality and justice has arrived. So there will be nothing for the messiah to do except to enjoy the messianic era!

I will end this answer with another story from our tradition. When a disciple of the rabbi of Lentscho visited the rabbi of Kotsk, his host said to him, "Give my greetings to your teacher. I love him very much, but why does he cry so much to God to send the messiah? Why does he not, rather, cry to mankind to turn to God?"

MR. SPONG: We have agreed to conclude the first exchange with the same question asked in both church and synagogue so that our answers can stand next to each other in immediate contrast. When Christianity began its historic life, it began within the bosom of Judaism, and it lived there for a period of time. What do you think happened two thousand years ago to split Christians and Jews apart into two hostile camps; and what, in your opinion, can we do about it today?

RABBI SPIRO: I disagree with you on the word *hostile,* because I am not sure that being in divergent camps necessarily breeds hostility. I think that we can maintain divergency without breeding hostility.

MR. SPONG: Our history is not very good.

RABBI SPIRO: No, the history is not really good, but perhaps the future can be better.

What happened two thousand years ago has not really changed. It is basically, once again, the crucial issue of your last question: Our major difference is in our radically different concepts of Jesus. Further, with the concept of Jesus, fundamental to our divergence is the meaning of *Christ.*

Jews can believe in Jesus. I believe in Jesus as a great man with prophetic capacities and magnetic powers. But we cannot believe in Christ, because the word *Christ* comes from the Greek *christos,* which means "messiah," and I have already indicated why this is a concept unacceptable to Jews.

What about Jesus himself, without the word *Christ?* Jesus was a faithful son of Israel, a faithful son of the synagogue, who sought not to destroy the law, which was the Torah, the five books of Moses, but who sought to fulfill those laws. As far as I can discern from reading the New Testament, he absorbed the moral laws and the ideals of his Hebraic environment. He did not consider his own teachings to be original, for he was deeply influenced by the prophets and the Psalms. He was a Jew when he proclaimed the fundamental gospel of love, which came from the Torah: "You shall love the Lord your God. . . . You shall love your neighbor as yourself." Jesus prayed Jewish prayers in the synagogue. He taught the basic values of Judaism, and there is nothing that I can disagree with in the Sermon on the Mount. Jesus was born of a Jewish family. His mother Mary's name was Miriam (Mary is a Greek word). His name in Hebrew was Joshua (Jesus is also a Greek word). His family arranged for his circumcision.

His diatribe against the money changers in the temple probably disturbed no one except the money changers themselves, because Jews of the time were quite accustomed to troublemakers; Isaiah, Jeremiah, Amos, and Ezekiel had all been troublemakers. Amos and Isaiah said: "I hate and despise your feasts." Jews were enjoying their feasts when these troublemakers rose to tell them that God despised what they were doing and enjoying! "Your new moons and your appointed seasons God also hates," Jeremiah said. "You are always shouting that the temple will save you. The temple is not sacred." A brand new idea. This young, rebellious upstart—and he was very young, probably under thirty—said to his people, who loved their temple and thought it inviolate, that the temple would not save them. "Your lives are sacred but only if you live justly." Like Jesus, Jeremiah was a troublemaker.

As a good Jew, Jesus made a pilgrimage to Jerusalem. To celebrate Passover in the holy city was the custom of all pious Jews. His last supper was the seder, the ritual meal of Passover itself. The martyrdom of Jesus was in keeping with Jewish history, especially at the time of the Roman persecutions, for Jews suffered many martyrs at that time and later. Rabbi Akiba, one of our greatest rabbis, was also one of our martyrs. He was tortured to death by the Romans in the arena. His skin was scraped off, leaving him to a slow, horrible, excruciating death.

We believe in the human Jesus. We believe in the Jewish Jesus. But he is not a prominent personality. In all of Judaism we do not have a single prominent personality. We de-emphasize personality itself, so that there is no chance of Judaism becoming a personality cult. Remember that wonderful tradition in the Book of Deuteronomy about the grave of Moses? We do not know where Moses is buried unto this day. That is how the Book of Deuteronomy ends, the reason being that the grave could not then become a shrine, and Moses himself would not be worshipped. Moses was a great man, but only a man, as was Jesus. Jesus was a great Jew, following nobly and courageously to the very end of his life the prophetic tradition. But he was a man. He was only human like Moses, Joseph, David, Jeremiah, and all of the great personalities of Jewish history.

And so in conclusion I would like to think in terms of trying to change the word *hostile* to *divergent* and of working together. The best response I can make to this problem, in spite of our radical differences, is a beautiful statement by a modern Jewish theologian, the late Abraham Joshua Heschel. He said that we are all born human beings, but life is a process of becoming human. I believe that this idea transcends our divergences, the hostilities of history, and everything else that separates us. We can come together, reconcile, and transcend our differences by recognizing and remembering that we are all human and that we are all children of the one God.

MR. SPONG: Thank you, Rabbi Spiro. I must add that we Christians do not know where the grave of Jesus is either, but to that discussion we will return in a subsequent session.

NOTE

1. See Chapter IV, pp. 47–52 and Chapter V, pp. 61–63.

chapter III

ON ONE FOOT: CHRISTIANITY

The dialogue sought to let Jewish people hear from a priest about the basic nature of Christianity.

RABBI SPIRO: Mr. Spong, you have intrigued me, as a Jew, with the startling title of your recent book, *This Hebrew Lord.* I can think of no better way to open this dialogue than to ask you how you came to the choice of that title.

MR. SPONG: Well, Rabbi Spiro, as much as I hate to admit it, the publisher actually gave it that title; but it was eminently satisfactory to me because it captured the central idea that I have tried to develop. It is a simple fact of history that Jesus was a Jew. It is rather amazing that so many Christians do not seem to understand that. He was raised the child of Jewish parents and nurtured in a Jewish home. He participated in all of the proper Jewish rituals: circumcision on the eighth day, presentation on the fortieth day, and Bar Mitzvah in Jerusalem when he was about twelve years of age. He worshipped the Jewish God Yahveh and observed in that worship all of the Jewish holy days. He studied the Jewish scriptures both at the feet of his parents and in the rabbinical schools, and I believe he came to understand his life totally in the light of those scriptures.

I came to the exciting conclusion that unless I could get inside the tradition that produced this life, I would never understand the one I call my Lord. No decision I have ever made has been so rewarding. For seven out of the last ten years of my life, I have submerged myself in a study of the Old Testament scriptures. In the process I have become a Hebrewphile. During the Six-Day War, I even preached while wearing a black patch over one eye.[1] I came to love my Jewish heritage in a very deep way. In Judaism I have found an attitude toward life, God, and history that has literally turned my Christian life around. I am deeply indebted to you. Judaism offered me a new and a fresh way to return to the central core of my Christianity.

So it is with Jewish eyes that I now look at my Lord. It is with Jewish understanding that I read the gospel. It is with Jewish accents that I proclaim the Christian message. My book, *This Hebrew Lord*, was an attempt to share with my readers this new vantage point.

Strangely enough, the Jesus of my childhood was so radically cut away from his Hebrew roots that I hardly thought of him as a Jew. The only pictures I ever saw portrayed him as a northern European with long, flowing blond hair and soft blue eyes. It was an unappealing, unmasculine portrait. As I was taught the Christian story in Sunday school, Jews were consistently pictured as villains. We Christians obviously have been insensitive through the ages to the anti-Semitism that we have perpetuated in so innocent a weapon as our Sunday school material. I would like to help right that wrong.

The Jesus of my childhood Christianity was not only Westernized and sentimentalized, but he also was covered over with the myth and superstition of the ages and with layer after layer of pious religion. In many ways this Jesus is not very attractive to secularized twentieth-century minds. Indeed, many modern people are so totally turned off by the image of Jesus that emanates from so many churches that they have given up both church and Christianity. This I know because I came very near to being one of them; and it was because of this that I was forced to seek my Lord in a new way—a fresh, believable way—or else resign my priesthood. It was that serious a faith crisis for me.[2] This led me to the process of looking at my Lord through Jewish eyes. I began to peel back the layers of religious tradition—the accretions of theological jargon, the distortions of the ages—and when I finished, I had discovered my Hebrew

Lord. It was a new angle for me and it produced a new insight. He was and is a Lord who satisfies my deepest intellectual curiosity and at the same time he is a Lord who is still understood completely within the bounds of what I believe to be orthodox Christianity.

If I said more than this, I would be giving a full book review; but this is how the book got its title, and this is a fair description of how I approach Christianity.

RABBI SPIRO: As I read the book I found myself alternately agreeing and disagreeing. My deepest agreement was with your discussion of *religion* and *secularity*. Would you discuss this?

MR. SPONG: I would be happy to, but I am not sure those words are the best ones to approach that subject. As you and I have both noted, there is no word in either ancient or modern Hebrew that can be translated accurately by our English word, *religion*. Religion is an aspect of life that has to do with holy things; and if that be so, then neither Judaism nor Christianity is properly called a religion. The God in the Bible is always a God of life; he is never a God of holy things. If religion is an activity of life, then we must assume that there is also an aspect of life that is nonreligious or secular. Even the use of *religion* to describe the arena of God's concern implies either that a portion of life lies outside God's concern or that life has no inherent holiness. This is to act as if God can be isolated into a ghetto called "religion." Personally, I find people who concentrate on religious things to be terribly boring. They always seem to have simplistic answers to life's complex questions, and oftimes they are unconcerned about life's great issues. If my ministry or my Christ have to be confined to the world of religion, then both ineffectiveness and pious play-acting are inevitable.

When Christianity left its Jewish origins, it entered the Greek world. Inevitably it confronted and adapted itself to the predominant Greek thought form of that day with its basic dualism that separated God from life, spirit from matter, the nonphysical from the physical. Holiness was gradually identified with the realm of the spirit, the nonphysical, the transcendent, leaving what remained to be profane, unholy and, finally, secular. This was the beginning of the division between religion and secularity. But it is not biblical.

In contradistinction to this false division stands the whole Jewish insight into life. The biblical narrative begins with the account of creation in which God pronounces every physical thing and life itself to be good. The Jewish nation begins with the historic exodus into freedom from the chains of slavery. That is life. There is nothing particularly religious about it.

This biblical insight is affirmed by the prophets who rose every time divine worship was separated from human justice, for worship that is not related to life is idolatry. In this tradition Jesus of Nazareth certainly lived. It was because God so loved the world, we Christians assert, that Jesus was born (John 3:16). And this Jesus did not say, "I have come to make you religious"; rather, he said, "I have come that you might have life and that you might have it abundantly" (John 10:10).

The God I meet in both the Old and the New Testaments is a God of life; he is never a God of religion. He is revealed in history, not in meditation. Indeed, religion seems to bore him as much as it bores me. In Isaiah God is portrayed as saying:

> Bring no more vain offerings;
>   incense is an abomination to me. . . .
>   I cannot endure iniquity and solemn assembly.
> Your new moons and your appointed feasts
>   my soul hates;
> they have become a burden to me,
>   I am weary of bearing them [1:13–14].

Religious things are not his concern, life is—all of life.

When God is assigned to the realm of religion, then the rest of life inevitably becomes "secular." It is separate and distinct from that which is sacred. This has produced, I believe, a modern distortion of both God and life. Today the realm of religion is so miniscule in importance that fewer and fewer people take it seriously. Simultaneously, secular life is so empty of any transcendent meaning that strange things are beginning to emerge that look like pseudoreligions. They range from drug experiences to oriental mysticism. When the holiness of God is separated from the center of life, neither God nor life will finally survive. In the classical Judeo-Christian tradition, as revealed in the biblical narrative, they are never separated.

This was the primary insight that gave me a clue to the method that I could and did use to recover my sense of God and my understanding of the Christ in the twentieth century. I did not have to search outside of life for the holiness and power of God; I would turn, rather, toward my world and discern with my newfound Hebrew eyes the God of life who reveals himself in history. I went back to the biblical attitudes among the Hebrew people and found that, in the worldly story of their biblical origins, many words we now interpret religiously had quite different meanings—words like *spirit, soul, spiritual, faith, sin, salvation, world, heaven, flesh,* and *Christ.*[3] Thus, this-world oriented biblical categories, not the traditional, pious, other-worldly religious categories became my starting place. I do not grieve today when I see *religion* declining, for the God I worship and the Christ I serve do not need religion to survive. Any God I now proclaim must be first and foremost the biblical God of life, and as such he will cut underneath the modern and false division between religion and secularity.

Incidentally, the title I originally submitted for my last book was "Jesus for the Nonreligious." That was unacceptable to my publisher, who feared it would be misunderstood and therefore offensive. Thus we agreed on *This Hebrew Lord.*

RABBI SPIRO: The point of my deepest disagreement with your book came when suddenly Yahveh of the Hebrew Bible became Christ of the New Testament. Would you share with us your understanding of the one you call the Christ?

MR. SPONG: This is, of course, the central issue that divides Christian and Jew and the issue that this dialogue must, at the very least, clarify. We cannot remove it.

I am a Christian because I believe that in Jesus of Nazareth

God was uniquely revealed to the world. Unfortunately, however, much of the verbiage we Christians use to portray our
Christ to the world is not biblical at all. For example, the Bible
never says, in a simplistic way, that Jesus is God. God is "wholly
other" in both the Old Testament and the New Testament.
Jesus, in the gospel, is shown praying to God. Obviously he is
not praying to himself. Jesus even uses the deeply intimate
Aramaic word *Abba* as his name for God.[4] We translate it
"Father." It might better be translated "dear Father" or "my
loving Father." Certainly in the mind of Jesus and in the minds
of the New Testament writers, Jesus and God were not identical.
Jesus was the Christ, and the Christ was the revelation of God,
even the essence of God. Because God was seen through Jesus in
a new way, it was impossible for Christians ever again to think
of God apart from Jesus or to think of Jesus apart from God.
This is the assertion of the New Testament. But a simple
identification between Jesus and God is not made. It would be
inaccurate both historically and theologically to portray the
Christian position as asserting that Jesus is God. Now, later in
Western Christianity, that assertion was made quite simplisti-
cally, even naively.[5] The best example was in the declaration
that Mary was "mother of God," but this is not biblical.

The Bible asserts that the power in Jesus was the power of
God, that God was in this Christ, that God was fully known in
this person, Jesus of Nazareth. We Christians believe that Jesus
was the "word of God" spoken to the world, that Jesus was the
"will of God" revealed to the world. We believe that in him and
through him God's power, God's life, God's love entered human
history in a unique way.

Therefore, from this Christian perspective, it was not a matter
of Yahveh of the Hebrew Bible becoming the Christ of the New
Testament. It was a matter of Jesus revealing the nature of
Yahveh in a new way, quite consistent with the Jewish tradition.
It was because we experienced the power of Yahveh in him that
we made the startling assertion: "You are the Christ."

When you and I, Rabbi Spiro, define God, we do so quite
similarly. You referred to the story of Moses at the burning

bush. Moses asked God's name, and God responded: "I am who I am" or "I will be who I will be." Here I believe, as you do, that God is defined biblically in terms of being. It is as if God is asserting: "I am the source of all that is. I am the ground of being." This concept comes closer to defining God than any other I know.

To me, God is the source of life, so the more deeply I live, the more I am in touch with God.

To me, God is the source of love, so the more freely I am able to love, the more I participate in his power.

To me, God is the ground of being, so the more fully I can be what I was created to be, the more God is revealed to me and in me.

Source of life. Source of love. Ground of being. That is what I believe God to be.

And what about Jesus? The Christian affirms that in this first-century Jewish life the fullness of God was experienced. The source of life was revealed in this one who was fully alive. The source of love was revealed in this one who was completely loving. The ground of being was revealed in this one who totally realized his potential.

He was open, full, free, and complete, so that nothing blocked the revelation of Yahveh in him. His life was God's word spoken in order to reveal God's meaning. His life lived out God's will in creation. He was completely what God created him to be, and his call to us is to discover his power and, in the strength of that power, to follow him. We follow him not by being like him, for then we would be creating a legalism; rather, we follow him by being all that each of us was created to be. This is what St. Paul means when he invites us to live "in Christ," and when he asserts that to be in Christ is to be "a new creation" (II Cor. 5:17). Paul believed the Christ to be the power of God to set human life free to be. This is also what John means when he says, "If the son has set you free, then you are free indeed" (8:36).

When I combine this truth with the new insight that arises for me when Jesus is placed in his Jewish setting, then I can see this Jesus more fully than I have ever seen him before. He is, for me, both a Jewish man and my Lord; or, in theological language, he is for me both a Hebrew Jesus and the Christian Christ. This understanding of Christianity is what I want to offer the world.

To me this Hebrew Lord is a magnificent union of both Jewish tradition and Christian affirmation. He is the full revealer of the God Yahveh in history, both Yahveh's word and his will. He is my Lord, my Savior: the Christ.

RABBI SPIRO: What was it that happened two thousand years ago that split Christianity from Judaism, and what can we do about it today?

MR. SPONG: The first Christians saw the revelation of God, in the person of Jesus, to be a new and fuller chapter of Judaism. Christianity was not to them a totally new thing. It was instead a new covenant, or new testament, intended not to replace but to add to the old covenant, or old testament. The disciples saw in Christianity a new branch of the ancient root of Jesse, but it was a branch that would move beyond Judaism and unify all mankind, overcoming the barriers of any racial or ethnic division. To share this meaning became a prime concern, so a sense of mission was immediately apparent in Christianity. That mission had to reach beyond Jerusalem, beyond Judea, and even beyond Samaria. It had to embrace, in Luke's words, "the uttermost parts of the earth." This meant that increasingly the Christian Church moved beyond Judaism and was destined to become a Gentile Church.

The first great struggle within the Church was whether Gentile converts must become Jews in order to become Christians (Acts 15). That conflict was decided in the negative: Jewish cultic practice was not required of Gentile converts, but the moral law of Judaism was. Armed with this compromise, Christianity exploded out of the bosom of Judaism into the Gentile world, carrying only Judaism's ethical demands. The more success Christianity had among the Gentiles, the greater the tension between Jews and Jewish Christians. Finally, the center of Christianity shifted from Jerusalem to Antioch, and the followers of Jesus began to use their new name, *Christians*. They were followers of him whom they called *Christos*. The Church was increasingly recognized as a Gentile body and identified as being separate and distinct from Judaism. This, incidentally, caused great problems for Christians, because Judaism was a legal religion in the Roman Empire. Christianity, as a new religion instead of a branch of Judaism, however, became immediately illegal and subject to persecution at the hands of the state.

When Jerusalem was destroyed by the Roman army in A.D. 70, the influence of Jewish Christians on the Christian Church was considerably lessened. Until 1948, the Jewish people of the world had to exist in exile without a homeland, a symbol of national identity; and increasingly the very survival of Jewish values depended on their remaining separate and distinct as a people. Thus anything which tended to blur their differences or that might lead to amalgamation was prohibited in Jewish circles. Christianity, at the same time, was committed to being the agent of a universal mission that would unite all mankind, and any barrier was something to overcome. So neither Jew nor Christian could be what they felt called to be in history without standing against the other. That seems to me to be a primary historic reason for the division.

What can we do about it today? I hope we are answering that question at this moment.

We can build mutual appreciation of each tradition, even where we are in fundamental disagreement as to what is finally true. We can affirm our unity in our origins and celebrate our common heritage. We can recognize the deep debt we each owe to the other. We can assert that underneath both our Jewishness and our Christianity there is a common humanity that we share with every racial and religious group in the world. Hopefully, that commitment to our oneness and our holiness as human beings is sufficient to cut the prejudice that seems to infect human hearts, even if it does not obliterate our differences. I, as a Christian, am called to that. You, as a Jew, are called to that. We begin in this much unity, and for that we can join in thanking Yahveh, our common God and our heavenly Father.

NOTES

1. The Israeli Defense Minister, Moshe Dayan, wore a black patch over one eye and seemed to be omnipresent during that moment of history.
2. The full story of this "faith crisis" is narrated in *This Hebrew Lord* (Seabury Press, 1974).
3. I have sought to spell out the biblical meaning of these words in *Honest Prayer* (Seabury Press, 1973) and *This Hebrew Lord.*
4. See *Honest Prayer*, Chap. 2, "Addressing God as Father."
5. Nowhere is this point more powerfully made than in John A. T. Robinson's book *The Human Face of God* (Westminster, 1974), where he demonstrates with the words of the Church fathers themselves that "orthodox" Christology has been docetic and not orthodox.

chapter IV

TO GROW IN HOLINESS

The dialogue sought to deepen the rabbi's exploration of Judaism.

MR. SPONG: In this session our purpose is to explore Judaism in more detail. We are not seeking a superficial level of agreement, nor are we planning a debate; we hope, rather, at the very least to be able to understand and appreciate the depth and beauty of this noble tradition. We hope to identify the wide area of common ground and common faith Christians and Jews share, while laying out our irreconcilable differences. Where there is no agreement, there can still be appreciation and understanding of the issues involved.

We begin, Rabbi Spiro, by asking you to explain how Judaism understands *sin;* and, in answering that, could you comment on the biblical view of the human condition as portrayed in the Genesis account of Adam and Eve?

RABBI SPIRO: To answer your question, we must go back to something more fundamental than the question of sin; Judaism's interpretation of the nature of human life itself. In the Hebrew Bible, the Old Testament, the features which characterize the Jewish mind are prominent. For example, there is no such thing as a perfect, flawless being. The great personalities in the Bible are all imperfect, blemished, or "sinful" in some way. Adam was blemished because of his disobedience. Noah was considered righteous only in comparison with his generation (Gen. 6:9). The rabbis of the Talmud suggested that had Noah been born in any other generation, his faults would have been evident, even glaring. Moses was not permitted to enter the promised land after forty years of leading his people through the wilderness, because he too was guilty of human shortcoming. The very human King David had his mind set on seducing Bathsheba and was thereby reprimanded by the prophet Nathan. Jacob, in his early life, was selfish and crafty, living on cunning. His name was changed to "Israel" after he wrestled with the angel; even though victorious, he was blemished by a physical limp.

No one in the Hebrew scriptures achieves perfection. Imperfect is the Bible's verdict on human nature. There is, therefore, no reason to denounce man because this existential condition is beyond his control. The Bible and Jewish tradition, therefore, are not saying to us that man is inherently sinful because he is depraved or lost. To the Jew, nothing about man is intrinsically evil—neither his soul nor his body. The human senses are to be developed and enjoyed. In fact, a great Jewish philosopher of the Middle Ages, Bachya Ibn Pakuda (1050–1120), said: "On the day of the judgment, man will be called to account for every innocent pleasure and joy that he has denied himself." The sex drive is good, according to the talmudic rabbis, and to this rabbi as well: It produces love, marriage, the family, and the perpetuation of humanity.

It follows, therefore, that sin is not the nature of man so much as it is an act, a deed of omission or commission. The Hebrew word *chatah*, "to sin," is the same word that is used when an archer stretches his bow, shoots an arrow, and misses the target. To sin is to miss the mark, to make a mistake. The mistake, of course, can be small and inconsequential or it can be enormous and destructive. The Garden of Eden account beautifully brings out this concept as an act. First, man, created *b'tselem Elohim*, "in the image of God," disobeyed God's law. God said in the story: "You must not eat of the tree of knowledge of good and evil" (Gen. 2:17). But Adam did eat of the tree. He disobeyed God. The sin, according to the talmudic rabbis, was man's knowledge transcending man's obedience to God's laws. This is the Hebrew equivalent of the Greek term, *hubris.*

In Hebrew we say *chutzpah:* a great arrogance on the part of man which then causes suffering, strife, misery, and bloodshed. Knowledge without wisdom is vacuous, and wisdom is the responsible application of knowledge. To sin, therefore, is to apply the gift of knowledge that God has given us in an irresponsible, unwise, unethical way, missing the mark set for us.

Even more important than the concept of sin is *teshuvah.* A poor but common translation of this word is "repentance." A better translation is "returning," "coming back"—to come back to one's true self as a human being, in the image of God. Judaism, a very practical, behavior-oriented tradition, asks: How do you come back to yourself? Our answer is, in several ways—through prayer, which is a deep meditation and concentration aimed at improving behavior; through acts of lovingkindness; charity, which has the power to change one's being; and through study, enlightenment, improving the mind. But the primary way is in *ma-aseh tov*, the good deed.

According to our tradition, the gates of *teshuvah*, of return, are always open to every person.

MR. SPONG: Sin is to miss the mark. The Greek word *hamartia* has that same connotation. The real issue is: If man is incapable of being what he was created to be, of living out his full potential, then to be human is to miss the mark or to "live in sin." This would appear to me to be saying that sin is a description of our being, not our doing. This becomes such a vital question because the way we understand sin determines the way we will both understand *savior.* I suspect that it is here even more than in the area of Christology that you and I find our deepest disagreement.

The role played in the Christian story of salvation by the one we call the Savior is directly determined by our understanding of the nature of human life. The basic question for us is whether or not the fullness of life and the image of God can be achieved by our deeds, by our righteousness, by knowing the truth and doing the truth, or whether some external power of love needs to embrace us wherever we are and whoever we are so that we are loved into the fullness of life and into the freedom of being.

Perhaps we can clarify this by looking at it from another angle. Paul, the great Christian missionary of the first century and the author of most of the epistles in the New Testament, was a Pharisaic teacher. He was, I gather from the biblical record, a strict constructionist. He diligently sought to obey the law, to achieve a life of righteousness; but his efforts produced, according to his own commentary, not love and life, but rigidity and external righteousness only. He said: "I know what I ought to do. I know the law, but I do not do it. And I know what I ought not to do, but I still do it" (Rom. 7). He concluded that if he did all righteous things—even giving his body to be burned at the stake of the martyr—but had not love, it profited him nothing (I Cor. 13). When he tried to face this aspect of his human experience, he was driven to this final question, which was framed in the Epistle to the Romans: "Who shall deliver me?" (7:24). Only when Paul asked this question did he see the meaning of the Christ, and his conversion resulted.

To clarify this issue, my question is: Assuming that one knows what is right or has learned what is right, where is the power in Judaism that enables one to do what is right? And where is it that you think Paul failed to understand that power, causing him thereby to leave Judaism for Christianity?

RABBI SPIRO: The answer to your question is not in the Bible but in the Talmud, the rabbinic literature that developed several hundred years beyond the life of Paul. The Hebrew Bible is simply not complete for Jews without the Talmud and other components of rabbinic literature. No Jew can understand the Bible apart from the entire spectrum of Jewish values and aspirations developed in talmudic and midrashic literature any more than the Old Testament is complete for Christians without the New Testament.

The power to do what is right comes from three sources.

First, the teaching-learning process. In Proverbs we find this statement: "Raise the child in the way that he should go, and he will never depart from it" (22:6). Identification with the Jewish tradition is a conditioning process that originates at birth. The advice is given in rabbinic literature that as a baby nurses at the breast, the mother should recite repeatedly: "Hear O Israel, the Lord, our God, the Lord is one." This will cause the child to have pleasant associations with this important biblical statement. The child starting to school should be given honey so that lessons are associated with sweetness. These are excellent examples of a form of behaviorism. Bar and Bat Mitzvah are marked with the reading of a passage from the Torah in Hebrew, making the act itself one of learning. Through this teaching-learning process, intensively carried out in the early years, the power and will to do what is right are burned into the consciousness.

The second source of power is revealed in the concept of *k'lal Yisrael,* the "community of Israel." Judaism *is* the community of Israel. By *Israel,* I do not mean the nation but the entire Jewish people. Judaism is a religion emphasizing communal identity and responsibility. The community's impact on the individual Jew is of great importance. Here the pressure to conform to the demands and expectations of the group is experienced. A Jew realizes himself most fully not in solitude but through sharing values and traditions with fellow Jews. Communal identity also relates to the concept of chosenness, *bechirah* in Hebrew. Being a member of the "chosen people" means living out the idea of *bechirah* through responsibility to the Jewish community. It is a community, not separate individuals, that is chosen by God to live out the ethical mandate enunciated in the Torah. The Torah is actually a constitution for the holy community. Exodus 19:6 states that the Jews should be a "kingdom of priests and a holy people." Nowhere does it say "holy individual." The command, "Be holy, for I the Lord your God am holy" (Lev. 19:12), is expressed in the plural, not in the singular: *K'doshim tih'yu.* The community imposes the high standards of living on the individual.

In the Book of Exodus, Moses asks God to identify himself.

God says *Ehyeh asher ehyeh*, "I will be who I will be" (3:14). This statement is explained in the Talmud to mean: " 'I will be who I will be' for individuals, but as for the community, I reign over them. If an individual decides to choose me, I shall be God for him; if he does not desire me, it is in his power to reject me. But as for the community, I will not permit them to reject me. The community is mine." In Jewish tradition, a worship service cannot be performed without a quorum of ten Jews, a *minyan.* This is not meant to be an arbitrary number; it is a theological concept assuring the individual of the experience of community. Community is so important in Judaism because it is the means of communicating values shared in common. The individual Jew, therefore, lives in and through the power of the community.

The existence, the welfare, the creative survival of the State of Israel is of utmost importance to Jews throughout the world not only because of the biblical heritage and its inextricable link to the promised land or because it is a haven for the persecuted and homeless, but primarily because it represents the indispensable value and ingredient in Judaism of communal solidarity.

The third source of power, which developed more fully after the lifetime of Paul, is expressed in the concept of *Shechinah.* This special and important term connotes the divine presence in human life, the immanence of God. The Talmud says: "The *Shechinah* is present wherever men gather to worship, where judges sit as a court, where justice is expressed, where a person helps another in need, where even one person studies Torah." In this context, *Ruach ha-Kodesh*, which means "holy spirit," is another important term. *Shechinah* and *Ruach ha-Kodesh*, are sometimes used interchangeably, because they refer to the manifestation of God in life, in the personal and intimate existence of every individual. This is the divine source of power which impels the Jew to do what is right.

Thus, through these three sources—the teaching-learning process, the force of the community itself, and the sense of God's presence—we are infused with the power to do what is right.

MR. SPONG: The Christian concept of holy spirit, basically, is the "giver of life"; so we would find agreement there. I think we might be able to characterize our disagreement as one of starting places. Jewish theology seems to me to start in "doing," hoping to create "being." Conversely Christian theology seems to me to start in the affirmation of "being" which hopefully will find expression in "doing." For Christians, the love that calls us into being is in the Christ, a power we find revealed in Jesus of Nazareth. It is of interest to note that this conflict not only divides Christianity and Judaism, but it was also a major issue in the Protestant reformation, using such words then as *grace* and *law*. Perhaps both approaches are aspects of eternal truth that can be kept alive only in tension.

Rabbi Spiro, how do you see the mission of Judaism? Is it to convert others to Judaism?

RABBI SPIRO: Modern Judaism is really not a proselytizing religion. There was a time when Judaism did proselytize and missionize. In late biblical and early post-biblical times, Jews were actually engaged in an active missionary program. We know from the historical writings of Josephus in the first century A.D. that when the Romans ruled over the entire Mediterranean world, Roman noblemen and their wives were attracted to the teachings of the Bible and of the rabbis. This missionary zeal came to an abrupt end, however, with the destruction of Jerusalem by the Romans in A.D. 70.

When that took place, Jews were more concerned about their own survival and preserving their heritage than about adding numbers to the Jewish fold. In fact, because of that great cataclysm in the year 70, it was a miracle that Judaism even remained alive. The rabbis actually began to discourage potential candidates by pointing out that being a Jew is a burden, not in terms of keeping the *mitzvot*, the moral and ritual commandments, but for social reasons. There was and is the real possibility that the person who becomes Jewish will encounter the whips and scorns of anti-Semitism.

It is a biblical concept that Judaism is the religion of all mankind. The Bible says: "Out of Zion shall go forth the Torah and the word of Yahveh from Jerusalem" (Mic. 4:2). I believe this statement is an explicit indication of missionary zeal, expressing the idea that the whole world will be influenced by this Torah emanating from Jerusalem. Even more explicit is the statement of Zechariah: "These are the words of the Lord of hosts: In those days, when ten men from nations of every language pluck up courage, they shall grasp the robe of a Jew and say, 'We will go with you because we have heard that God is with you' " (8:23). The phrase "ten men" may refer to the idea of *minyan*, which I mentioned earlier. The *minyan* is a symbol of community; that is, the community of every nation throughout the world would be asserting: We shall go with you because we have learned about your amazing God, Yahveh, and we want to attach ourselves to you and your beliefs.

Another missionary concept which developed around the same time is expressed by the exilic prophet, calling Israel to be an *or la-goyim*, "a light unto the nations" (Isa. 42:6). The purpose was not to mass-manufacture Jews, but to generate peace, justice, and love through Jewish values. He was saying that the Jewish people will be a light to the nations of the world, calling all peoples to justice, love, righteousness, and universal peace. The prophet did not mean that everyone should become Jewish.

This same note is sounded in the liturgy that we recite at the annual seder dinner of the Passover festival, expressed in the Hebrew phrase *tikkun olam*, "improving the world." Every Sabbath we read in our prayer book that we must work and pray for the day when "the Lord shall be one and his name shall be one." While each Jew is a part of a Jewish community, he is also a part of the world community. Our prayer book goes even further, admonishing us to have "regard for other men's faith."

The universalism of Jewish tradition is expressed in the statement: "All the righteous people of every nation shall inherit the world-to-come." This means that every righteous person deserves a place in God's world. The rabbis asked: Who is righteous? What are the criteria for being righteous? "All human beings who follow the laws of Noah" was their answer. Because

Noah lived before Abraham, the first Jew, the laws of God's covenant with Noah were universal, applying to all mankind, regardless of race, religion, creed, nationality, or any other distinction. The seven basic Noachian laws prohibit idolatry, murder, theft, blasphemy, incest, eating the flesh of a living animal, and conclude by demanding the promotion of justice. Those who observe these fundamental laws of humanity are known as *b'nay Noah*, sons of Noah, and they deserve God's blessing. The implication is unequivocal: A non-Jew does not have to convert in order to merit salvation. This expresses the hope that all human beings will come to God, the universal God of all men revealed through the seven laws of Noah.

MR. SPONG: St. John would not be far from that when he stated that God is love and whoever abides in love abides in God. And St. Luke, in the song sung by Simeon, states that the Christ is to be "a light to lighten the Gentiles and the glory of Israel."

Could we move to the category of revelation. In the Jewish mind, how does God reveal his will in history?

RABBI SPIRO: Again, I must refer to the Talmud. The Book of Leviticus says: "I will be your God, and you will be my people" (26:12). Commenting on this verse, the Talmud says that Yahveh can become Israel's God only if Israel really becomes his people. Elsewhere in the Talmud, allegorical but nonetheless instructive, it is written: "Prior to Abraham, God was only in the heavens; but Abraham brought him down to earth through his righteous deeds and made him sovereign of the whole earth." These passages imply that God is revealed in man's emulation of God's attributes and deeds. But note, it is attributes, not essence, that is revealed. Both the Hebrew Bible and the post-biblical literature of Judaism resist any other kind of revelation. The Book of Leviticus sums it up by saying: "You shall be holy for I am holy." God is perceived primarily in sacred actions which we are to emulate. The Talmud asserts that God himself cares for the widow and orphan, visits the sick, teaches Torah, and engages in acts of holiness. God is revealed, therefore, through deeds which express his divine will. By acting out the "image of God" in our lives, we perceive him and reveal him in the world.

We grow in holiness through the performance of the laws of the Torah. In so doing, we learn more about God himself. Revelation is thus a progressive process as we deepen our understanding of ourselves and accept the responsibilities we have for others in the world.

This is the behavioral orientation of Judaism. Jeremiah says: "Let him that glories, glory in this: that he understands intelligently that I am the Lord who exercises mercy, justice, and righteousness in the earth" (9:24). A talmudic rabbi, musing over how a person could understand God intelligently, concluded that it was by emulating his attributes. Jeremiah further states: "He judged the cause of the poor and needy; then it was well. Is this not to know me? says the Lord" (22:16). A great Jewish philosopher, Hermann Cohen (1842–1918), wrote: "Only the effects of his essence does God want to reveal to Moses, not his essence itself."

This idea is expressed succinctly in the first of the Ten Commandments: "I am the Lord your God who brought you forth from the land of Egypt, out of the house of bondage" (Exod. 20:2). The "I am" phrase—the being and nature of God—is incomprehensible without the action phrase, "who brought you forth." God acts. His deeds in the world, his activity in history, are the continual process of bringing redemption and freedom to his own humanity. This is how we know him. This is how he reveals himself to us.

MR. SPONG: It is at this point that I am always surprised that it is not Christology that divides us as significantly as we might have thought. The Christian affirmation about Jesus of Nazareth is that in human history one, in fact, emulated God's acts or deeds perfectly and therefore reveals him in a new way as God's word to the world.

There is a question about which we Christians need to be sensitized. You have already mentioned that within Judaism

God is viewed as having made a moral commitment to the covenant relationship. I wonder if you would share with us how you think the horrors of World War II, particularly the anti-Semitism in Nazi Germany, affected the contemporary Jewish attitude toward God's moral commitment in the meaning of God's covenant with his people.

RABBI SPIRO: A contemporary theologian, Richard Rubenstein, wrote in a book entitled *After Auschwitz* that the thin line between God and man was severed in the Nazi concentration camps in Europe. He was referring to what we have come to call "Holocaust," a feeble word to describe the indescribable, unimaginable horrors of the Second World War. Holocaust—the murder of six million innocent Jews—seemed to Rubenstein, and obviously to others, to sever the relationship between God and man, even to have caused the "death of God." It is difficult to believe that an all-good and all-powerful God would allow such unfathomable evil and suffering.

I find this theology unacceptable and naive. One must look at the Holocaust in terms of historical, economic, and political reality, not in theological terms alone, to determine why six million Jews were wantonly killed. Sophisticated technology was available to the Nazis to enable them to annihilate so many people. Rubenstein's theology is unsophisticated because sheer *numbers* should not be important as a theological consideration. A theological position cannot develop on the basis of quantification. What is the critical number that determines the death of God—one? one hundred thousand? one million? six million?

The Bible does not refer to numbers when dealing with evil in relation to God. There are no mass murders in the Bible which prompt disturbance about theodicy. In spite of slaughters by either palace revolution or foreign invasion, the biblical emphasis still is on the struggle of one man, like Job, and the poignant account of his personal suffering. The Bible focuses on Cain's murder of Abel—one individual destroying another human life. The Garden of Eden story suggests that man succumbs to sinfulness when his knowledge outstrips his obedience to God's law. From this ethical perspective of Judaism, knowledge without allegiance to God's will is dangerous. Knowledge without obedience caused the expulsion from the garden.

During the 1930s in Nazi Germany, there was a higher percentage of Ph.D.s than in any other country. Here was great knowledge without moral sensitivity, which enabled the state to transcend justice and disregard mercy.

Those who say that God is dead because of Auschwitz and Dachau are naive. If that view be adopted, God should have died long ago. He should have died when the Romans destroyed Jerusalem and razed the temple, or at the time of the inquisition, or during the European crusades. He should have died on any other occasion when human life was wantonly tortured or savagely slaughtered—Biafra, Vietnam, or Watts.

If quantification is the issue, where do we draw the line between human responsibility and divine responsibility? My answer is that the heavens belong to God, and the earth belongs to man. God created the earth, but he gave it to us to cultivate. This is our earth to tend and to love. The earth is inhabited by human beings whose responsibility is to make it a good world. God gave this responsibility freely, lest we be puppets and not human at all. Our freedom to choose, combined with the extremely sophisticated technology of Nazi Germany and the efficient bureaucratic structure that constructed the death camps, determined the extent of Nazi brutality. This went far beyond Cain and Abel in quantification, but not in terms of the death or denial of God. Cain's murder of Abel repudiates God just as much as did the Holocaust, if indeed murder is a reason for repudiation or denial at all.

MR. SPONG: In closing, I focus on our area of deepest agreement. You have stated that the most satisfactory definition of God for you is in terms of being, in conjunction, of course, with the idea of doing. Would you explain that further?

RABBI SPIRO: We go to the Hebrew word *Yahveh*, to which we have referred numerous times. This name means "one who causes to be" or "one who calls into being." In my reading I have never found a concept of God superior to the fullness of meaning in this name. In the grammatical structure of the word Yahveh, God is not "being" alone. He is the *power* of being. The word is constructed according to the causative form of the verb *to be*. In the famous Exodus story where God confronts Moses and says that while he has been known as *El Shaddai* (God of Power), Moses shall say to his people: "Ehyeh (I will be) has sent me unto you" (3:14). Both *Yahveh* and *Ehyeh* are in the future tense, implying that God should be understood in terms of both the power to be (causing to be) and the power to become. God is thus always understood as being in the process of becoming more powerful, more loving, and more just. God is creating more, being more, and prompting us—his creatures—to become more than we are.

This concept is affirmed by the first verb of the Bible: *bara*, "he (God) created." The first chapters of Genesis depict the Hebraic view of reality, which is reflected in many phrases and terms. The being of God is always in the future-oriented process of creating, becoming, acting. God is the power calling life into ever-greater being. In grammatical parlance, we say that the past tense is the "perfect" and the future tense is the "imperfect." In this sense I would say that God is "imperfect," in that he is the power of becoming—he is future-oriented, goal-directed, always in process, and generating the same dynamic in his creatures who reflect his image.

Jewish literature corroborates this idea of a continuous creation. One statement from the prayer book says: *Uv-tuvo m'chadesh b'chol yom tamid ma-aseh b'raysheet*—"In his goodness God continues unceasingly to express his creative power." The Talmud enjoins us, in the presence of the wonders of nature, to offer this benediction: "Blessed art thou, O Lord . . . who performs the wonders of creation." The verb is not in the past tense; God is always in the process of performing creative wonders.

This idea is the theme of an ancient controversy. The schools of Shammai and Hillel (first century A.D.) argued about the benediction over the lights, which comes to the conclusion of the

Sabbath ritual. Shammai would say, "Blessed art thou . . . who created the lights of fire." But Hillel contended that it should be: "Blessed art thou . . . who creates the lights of fire." Hillel won the argument, because it is basic to Jewish thought that God is always engaged in the process of creation.

Rabbi Bunam, a great Hasidic leader (d. 1827), says: "The Lord created the world in a state of beginning. The universe is always in an uncompleted state, in the form of its beginning. It is not like a vessel which the master works to finish; it requires continuous labor and *renewal by creative forces.* Should these cease for only a second, the universe would return to primeval chaos."

A midrash says that God created all things in the first six days of creation, but he did not make them perfect. His task, therefore, is the continuous process of improving the universe, leading it toward perfection, which is an infinite task. The world is not a finished product, and it never will be. God likewise will never be finished. He continues to create a world which displays the glorious evidence of law and harmony, of dynamism and growth, of being and becoming.

MR. SPONG: Your answer reminds me of my favorite verse in the New Testament. It is found in Jesus' words from the Johannine literature and sums up for me the purpose of my Christ: "I have come that you might have life and that you might have it in all of its fullness" (John 10:10). We seem to agree on the ultimate goal. Our disagreement is on the means necessary to achieve that goal. Perhaps both our agreements and disagreements will become more obvious as we explore the Christian gospel more intensively in our next session.

chapter V

TO GROW IN GRACE

The dialogue sought to deepen the priest's exploration of Christianity.

RABBI SPIRO: What do you, as a Christian, mean by *sin* and *original sin?*

MR. SPONG: I know of no place where biblical meanings are more distorted than in the definition of such terms as *sin* and *original sin.* Layer after layer of ecclesiastical dogma have given these words moralistic interpretations so that most people are conditioned to think of them in terms of deeds. This is unfortunate because the way one defines sin determines the approach one must take to overcome sin. When Christians define the role of the Savior, inevitably a particular view of sin is presupposed. In like manner, the Jewish concept of the law assumes a particular concept of sin. The way each of us defines sin grows out of our particular understanding of humanity. I suspect that we will find here an area of profound disagreement.

I was a priest in the Episcopal Church for five years before the impact of the gospel broke into my conscious mind. This happened when I began to understand the biblical meaning in words like sin and original sin.

The psalmist says: "In sin hath my mother conceived me" (51:5); that is, when I was conceived, I entered the reality of sin. That could not possibly mean an evil deed. The Torah itself reminds us that the "sins of the fathers are visited upon the children to the third and fourth generation" (Exod. 20:5). Again, this must go beyond the simplistic cause and effect level of human behavior. The early Christian practice of the baptism of infants was for "the forgiveness of sin." By every moralistic standard, the baby has not yet committed evil actions, so this reference must point to something deeper than the level of behavior. Rabbi Spiro, you have said that the Hebrew word used for sin means "to miss the mark." That same note is found in the New Testament Greek word for "sin": *hamartia.* But "to miss the mark" to me means not to do a bad deed but, rather, to fail to be what one was created to be. Sin is thus a description of our humanity. It is a universal aspect of all human experience.

As human beings, we live with our limitations, always judging ourselves by the dream of what we yearn to be. The resulting gulf is the valley of our discontent which feeds the universal human feelings of inadequacy, insecurity, inferiority. It is here that self-rejection and self-negativity arise. Every human being needs a love that is beyond what any of us receives. Hence, our humanity reveals a brokenness—a distortion. We see it in our insatiable ego needs: our attempts to demonstrate our worth and even our compelling necessity to prove that we possess a superior truth, a superior God. This self-centeredness lies underneath our behavior and constantly emerges in our deeds. This insight into humanity is what the Bible attempts to capture and describe in the word sin and the concept original sin. Biblical sin is a description of our being, not our doing. It is ontological, not moral.

Thus Isaiah can say: "All we like sheep have gone astray" (53:6)—astray from our human destiny to be full and free and whole. The psalmist can say: "In the human condition of sin we are conceived and born" (51:5). The Torah can speak of the sins of the fathers that transcend the generation, for out of our inadequacy and insecurity we do twist and warp our children, and they in turn twist and warp their children.

It is because a child enters the distorting world of inadequate love at birth that we Christians baptize our infants for "the forgiveness of sin." In that process we hope to relate each child to the healing power of God which is beyond our human capacity to create.

Sin, then, is our inability to live fully because of the inadequacy of the love that we have received, thus making us incapable of being what we most deeply are: whole, free persons who reflect the image of God. When we see sin in this biblical light, we know that it is beyond the power of rules, good advice, good examples, or even the law. If this is sin, then the function of the law is to minimize the hurt by setting rules to govern the behavior of broken, distorted human beings. The law is necessary, given the nature of humanity, but it does not and it cannot produce life, for it cannot create love. This is why we Christians look beyond the law for the external power of love that can affect the being of humanity and thus transform that human nature out of which all our deeds flow. Sin, understood in terms of being rather than doing, is the concept that underlies my presentation of the gospel.

RABBI SPIRO: Would you then explain what you, as a Christian, mean by *messiah* and *salvation?*

MR. SPONG: Messiah is the restorer of creation and the revealer of God. *Messiah* is a word used to describe any life through which God is experienced in time and history. Whenever love touches life in its sinful condition and creates being, there messiah is seen.

The Hebrew concept of messiah is translated *christos* in Greek, and from that we get the word *Christ.* The word Christ does not refer to a person; it is a concept. It is the power of God experienced in human history. It is love creating life, restoring creation, and breaking shackles that bind and distort our humanity. It is inaccurate to call the Christian Lord "Jesus Christ." He is Jesus in whom we see the power of Christ.

Christpower is, however, not limited to Jesus of Nazareth. Because it is the revelation of God, it shares in the eternity of God, stretching into infinity on both sides of the thirty-year life of Jesus of Nazareth. Obviously, God made himself and the power of his love known to man before the life of Jesus. Christpower is seen in every covenant described in the Hebrew scriptures: covenants with Adam, Noah, Abraham and with Moses at Mount Sinai. Christpower is seen in every prophet who opened people's eyes to the presence of God in the midst of the world. It is seen in the human yearning for wholeness that fed every Old Testament messianic dream. Christpower also continues to be revealed in human history far beyond the time of Jesus. Wherever love is experienced, humanity is achieved, barriers are overcome, and community is created; there Christpower is experienced, messiah is revealed.

In the Hebrew scriptures, there were many images of the messianic role. Some were corporate and some were individual. They ranged from a mighty, earthly deliverer to the humble servant figure of Second Isaiah. Some seemed to have only human origin, such as the one who would rise from the root of Jesse; others seemed to be endowed with heavenly power like the Son of Man in the Book of Daniel. Some envisioned a universal reign of peace that was quite external; others anticipated an internal peace—a peace that passes understanding. Yet behind every image, the messianic function was to fulfill creation, redeem life, and bring freedom and wholeness to humanity. The messiah was to usher in the kingdom of God and do the work which only the love of God could accomplish.

It was when the disciples glimpsed this power in the life of Jesus of Nazareth that they made the startling and unique messianic claim for him. Peter voiced this at Caesarea Philippi: "Jesus, you are the Christ" (Mark 8:29). That is, "Jesus, in you we see and experience the presence of God. You bring to us the gifts of God: love, life, and being. To bring these gifts is to be messiah. You are the Christ."

To be a Christian, one must make an exclusive claim for the power of Christ but not an exclusive claim for Jesus of Nazareth. Christians do not necessarily claim that Jesus is the only revealer of God. Even the claim in the fourth gospel, "No one comes to the Father but by me" (John 14:6), is not as exclusive as it appears. This gospel is not a biography of the Jesus of history. It is a theological treatise on the power of the Christ that is revealed in the life of Jesus of Nazareth.

The fourth gospel does not pretend to record the actual sayings of the historic Jesus. This is best seen in the "I am" sayings of this gospel. It is a worshipping Church that has experienced Christ in Jesus of Nazareth who records Jesus as saying, "I am the bread of life"; "I am the living water"; "I am the good shepherd." So when the author of the fourth gospel asserts that "no one comes to the Father but by me," he means by "me" the power of Christ which was seen in Jesus. This is the power through which we all come to the Father, but clearly Jesus of Nazareth is not the only expression of this Christ or of this Christpower. Christians assert only that Jesus is the Christ for us because everything we know God to be, we have found in him. The love, the life, and the being, that is, the Christpower found in Jesus, meets us at the level of our sin and calls us to a new life in him. Here we are freed to be ourselves and hear the call to love others in his name. Here our potential is ignited, and we are compelled to share ourselves with the world. This is salvation. But, true to the God of the Hebrew scriptures, to know Christpower is not to be religious; it is to be whole, to be free, to be fully human. We discern, celebrate, and reveal the holiness of God in every human encounter.

This love does not require every person to accept our particular understanding of this Christpower as the only possibility of salvation. It does require that we share this love with every person so that we become agents of life, calling others into expressions of their own unique being. There can be no arrogance in the Christian gospel when it is properly understood. There can be no sense of inferiority and superiority in our witness. There is no demand that my creed be the only creed or that my words be the only words that can interpret every human experience of God. Jesus placed a single command on his disciples: "As I have loved you," he said, "so love one another" (John 15:12). To give love is to share salvation with the world.

That is to live out the meaning of messiah. That is the power of Christ that we Christians find in Jesus of Nazareth.

RABBI SPIRO: The center of Christianity seems to be the Easter story. Resurrection is a difficult concept, even unbelievable, to so many today. How would you, as a Christian, explain the resurrection?

MR. SPONG: There is no doubt that the Easter event is the central moment in the Christian story. It is to the Christian what the Exodus is to the Jew. It was in Easter for Christians and in the Exodus for Jews that each of us came into being as distinct and separate people, chosen to perform a particular vocation as the people of God in history. That election was never an election to privilege for either of us, though in our weakness, both of us have at times so interpreted it. It was, rather, an election to service, a call to be bringers of light into the world.

I do not know how to measure the objective external event we Christians call the "resurrection." All I can say is that the disciples were deeply and intensely aware of the presence of their living Lord after his death, and this awareness possessed fantastic power. Because of whatever Easter was, the disciples who had been hiding out in a locked and barred upper room, fearful of their lives, were emboldened to risk their necks, to endure persecution, and finally to die the death of martyrs. They did this not only without fear, but with an incredible sense of joy. Because of whatever Easter was, these Jewish disciples, taught from birth to worship only God, found the presence of God so complete in Jesus of Nazareth that they no longer could see God apart from this Jesus, nor could they see Jesus without simultaneously seeing God. Jesus thus became one who mediated God to them in a unique way, and this forced them, almost against their will, to include him in their act of worship, acknowledging that this was life-changing power.

Because of whatever Easter was, a new holy day was created: the first day of the week. The Christian Sunday was the Day of the Resurrection; it was not the Jewish Sabbath of rest, though in later history the two days were so confused that many

Christians today think Sunday is to be observed by refraining from labor—a totally nonbiblical idea. No Sunday closing laws can be grounded in the New Testament.

The objective, external details of Easter are the subject of much debate. Even the gospel writers disagree on details. That something of incredible power happened, however, is beyond question, for a mighty force was born on that day that was destined to conquer the Roman Empire in three hundred years and to dominate Western civilization for two thousand years.

When I speak of the internal reality or subjectivity of the resurrection, I can do so with more precision; for at the very least, Easter was that moment when suddenly it dawned on the disciples that Jesus brought to them the power to live, the grace to love, and the courage to be. In that moment they experienced God's love in a new way, for this love embraced them and freed them to be themselves. They realized that though they had denied, betrayed, abandoned, and misunderstood this Jesus, he loved them still. He loved them not because of—or on the level of—their doing, but simply because they were who they were: children of God. Easter was the moment when this love touched them, calling them to live and empowering them to love. On the internal level, then, Easter was not just the resurrection of Jesus, it was the resurrection of the disciples: a resurrection from their universal, broken, insecure humanity into a new fullness of life and a new courage to be, a new freedom and wholeness. Paul understood it this way, for he wrote "if anyone is in this Christ, he is a new creation" (II Cor. 5:7).

This life power was and is so real to Christians that in its presence the power of death shrinks into insignificance. For when one has tasted real life, experienced complete love, dared to be a whole person, then one has touched that which is eternal, and death no longer possesses fear. I believe in resurrection, both within life and beyond life, because I believe that the God of life has called and enabled me to live, now and forever. Recognition of that call and empowerment comes for me through a first-century Jew named Jesus of Nazareth—hence, he is my Christ.

My mission as a Christian is to share that power and to give of that love as I have received it, and thus to be an agent of life. I am not called to demand that others concur with my words or my understandings, but only that my Christ be shared. But let it be very clear that my Christ is not my theology, but my experience of the life, the love, the being of God. So I am called as a Christian to be who I am, letting the power in that alone be my witness. If in doing that, resurrection is experienced by another on his terms, inside his heritage, then I can only say, "Thanks be to God."

RABBI SPIRO: Previously, you have made the point that Jesus was a Jew and therefore must be understood within that tradition, and yet your New Testament seems to me to deny this reality with stories of his miraculous birth which suggest that not only was he not Jewish, he was not even human. Would you comment on this?

MR. SPONG: The birth narratives in the New Testament are limited to Matthew and Luke, and they represent a rather late development of Christian tradition. Mark, the earliest gospel, written about A.D. 65, presents no hint of miraculous birth. Paul, who did all of his writing between A.D. 49 and 64, never alludes to a miraculous birth tradition. John, the last gospel to be written, is obviously aware of the birth traditions of both Matthew and Luke; and he specifically chooses to ignore them, if not to deny them. It is important to state that in my mind Mark, Paul, and John present the most exalted understanding of the Christ in the New Testament.

I do not regard the birth narratives as historic, and most New Testament scholars that I know, both Catholic and Protestant, do not either. The birth narratives are not a prerequisite to seeing Jesus as the Christ. If we literalize the birth narratives, we destroy the deepest Christian claim about Jesus, namely, that in the fullness of Jesus' humanity the fullness of God's power is experienced. If he is not completely human, this claim cannot hold.

We should also be aware that birth narratives are all

legendary. No one waits outside a hospital or a house for a great person to be born. People become great first, and then that moment they entered history becomes significant. It is never the other way around.

The formation and existence of birth narratives indicate that the adult life of the subject had a major impact which human categories were insufficient to measure. This becomes very clear as we analyze the way in which the traditions developed in both Matthew and Luke, for they were quite different.

Matthew was writing to the Hellenized Jews of the dispersion, and he opened his gospel with an interpretive portrait painted with great finesse and beauty. He filled that portrait with images which he drew from Jewish tradition, from popular history, and from his own fertile imagination. The author of this book at no time considered these opening chapters to be literal prose. He knew that he was deliberately creating a portrait with his use of symbol and poetry.

His gospel began with a carefully constructed genealogy that he forced into an artificial symmetry by conveniently forgetting some of the generations. To his Jewish readers this made the point that Jesus was of Davidic lineage, a prerequisite in popular messianic thinking.

Then Matthew moved into the core of his account of the virgin birth. Miraculous birth legends began to circulate among Christian communities late in the first century as an attempt to explain the origin of Jesus' power. Matthew knew these traditions, and he searched the scriptures in order to find a clue that would unlock this mystery. Unfortunately, Matthew, in the preparation of his gospel, used the Greek translation of the Old Testament, the Septuagint. In this version he found a verse in Isaiah that proclaimed: "A virgin shall conceive and bear a son, and his name will be Immanuel" (7:14). Matthew pounced on that verse with all the fervor of a fundamentalist preacher and wrenched it out of context and used it as the basis for his virgin story.

The Greek word translated "virgin" is *parthenos,* and indeed does contain the connotation of virginity. However, when we go behind the Greek translation to the Hebrew text, we discover that *parthenos* translates the Hebrew word *almah,* which means simply a "young woman." There is no connotation of either virginity or nonvirginity in this Hebrew word. If the author of Isaiah had wanted to use the Hebrew word for virgin, he would have used *betulah.* This means that the story of the virgin birth in Matthew is built on a connotation to a text that exists only in the Greek translation and not in the Hebrew at all.

Even more questionable does the verse become when it is placed in its historic context in Isaiah. Here Ahaz, king of Judah, was under severe pressure from Pekah, king of Israel, and Rezin, king of Syria, to join them in a common defense against the Assyrians. Should Ahaz refuse, they threatened to march on Jerusalem, overthrow Ahaz, and place on the throne of Judah a more cooperative king. On the other hand, if Ahaz joined this anti-Assyrian coalition, he would incur the wrath of the Assyrians, who had the power to destroy all of these little nations with a minimal effort. Isaiah advised Ahaz to remain aloof from Pekah and Rezin, whom he called "smoking fire-brands," and to place his trust in Yahveh. Instead, Ahaz appealed to Assyria for support against the legions of Pekah and Rezin, who immediately moved militarily on Jerusalem. With a siege being imminent, Ahaz toured the city to check his defenses and to reassess his situation. Isaiah confronted him and promised a sign that would convince him that God would protect his nation. That sign was that a young woman would give birth to a child, and, continued Isaiah, before this child was grown the kingdoms of Pekah and Rezin would be desolate. Through no stretch of the imagination could this be a reference to the birth of a messiah almost eight hundred years later. Matthew, however, ignored the context and accepted the connotation "virgin," which is in the Greek translation only; and he made this text support the legends of miraculous birth that were circulating among Christians. Indeed, one must wonder whether this misunderstood text created the particular form the birth legends took.

Matthew also borrowed from Jewish tradition the account of

a star in the heavens that announced the birth of Isaac, the child of promise, and Moses, the great deliverer. By the use of this star in his narrative, he could claim for Jesus the twin accolades, "child of promise" and "great deliverer."

He then reached into popular history and captured an episode that occurred in Rome some forty years before Matthew wrote. This event was recorded by the Roman historian, Pliny, and obviously was well known. It had to do with oriental visitors journeying to Rome to pay homage to the emperor Nero. These visitors, it is recorded, returned home by a different route. Matthew wove this into his interpretive portrait and through it proclaimed that the life about which he was now writing was in fact the king of the universe. Then, to make sure his readers did not miss his point, he had them present this babe with highly symbolic gifts—gold, the mark of a king; frankincense, the mark of a god; and myrrh, the mark of suffering and death.

Finally, Matthew completed his magnificent portrait with a feature that his Jewish audience would immediately recognize. He told the story of Herod's soldiers going to Bethlehem to kill Jewish male babies just as the Egyptian pharaoh had moved to kill Jewish male babies, years before. In the Egyptian massacre, Moses was spared to become the great deliverer; so now Jesus, the new Moses, is similarly spared.

In this manner Matthew alerts his Jewish readers to listen to the story of Jesus who is presented as the son of David, the sign of God, the child of promise, the great deliverer, the new Moses, and the power of Yahveh. He did in poetry what mere prose could never accomplish; but, if one literalizes it, the narrative will not survive.

Luke seems to have a somewhat different origin for his birth narrative, but it is obviously no more historic or literal. Chapters one and two of Luke are quite different from the bulk of his gospel, possessing a different style and even a different vocabulary. They are filled with semitic phrases and with references to early Jewish history that would not be familiar to Luke's Gentile readers. There are references made to Jewish worship practices with no clarifying explanation. These facts cause scholars to speculate that the opening chapters were added probably by Luke to his already completed work, but that they had a previous literary history.

An internal analysis of Luke's first two chapters also reveals a highly liturgical flavor with at least four hymns of praise containing an interpretation of the full adult life and death of this child Jesus. These hymns have a specific meter and rhythm and are still used in liturgical churches throughout the world. We note further that the Lucan birth narrative is told in a series of self-contained scenes—tableaux—that together interpret the power of the Christ. I have studied these narratives for years without putting together what now seems so obvious to me. These stories are totally familiar to most of us because we have seen them dramatized as a pageant each year in our churches. They seem so easy to dramatize. The reason, I am now convinced, is that they were created for dramatization. The first two chapters of Luke were originally a liturgical pageant created in Palestine among Jewish Christians to celebrate not so much the birth of Jesus as his life and power. Their unknown, original author did not intend them to be literalized. This was a play. Luke discovered it, was charmed by it, and added it to his gospel with little or no editorial change, keeping even the semitisms and the references to Jewish history.

When the account is analyzed, the scenes become obvious, each complete and designed for easy staging.[1] Thus, just as Matthew presented an interpretive portrait, Luke offered a dramatic pageant to herald the birth of a man in whose adult life God had been revealed.

The birth narratives were developed to say that the power in Jesus of Nazareth was beyond human capacity to produce. We Christians believe this, even when we recognize the details to be legendary. I love these birth narratives, but only because I am free to see the beauty, joy, romance, and profundity which lie underneath their literal form.

RABBI SPIRO: In the second chapter of Mark, Jesus attributes to himself the prerogative of forgiving sins. What is the source of his authority?

MR. SPONG: It is important to state, first of all, that we can never be sure of the accuracy of the quotations that the gospel writers attribute to Jesus. To our knowledge Jesus left no written records at all. The earliest gospel, Mark, was completed some thirty-five years after the first Easter. Luke and Matthew are both generally dated around A.D. 85, and John as late as A.D. 110. With the possible exception of John, which is a completely different kind of book, all of the gospels lean heavily upon an oral tradition that was shaped and formed in living congregations. Most of the isolated episodes that we have recorded in Matthew, Mark, and Luke floated freely according to the needs of the local Christian communities. In that state they quickly lost their historic time-place context. The episodes were very much like ornaments on a Christmas tree: Each is beautiful in its own way and can be placed anywhere on the tree without affecting its integrity. If Mark had written his gospel a year later, the order of his episodes could well have been totally different. The one exception to this rule is the passion narrative; that is, the events which begin with the Palm Sunday procession into Jerusalem and culminate in the story of the cross. This narrative seems to have achieved its complete written form very early and to have been treasured to the point of memorization by every local congregation.

The gospel writers arranged the other episodes in the narrative according to their skeleton outline: They knew that Jesus began his career in Galilee, ended it in Jerusalem, and had to get from one to the other. That is the basic outline of Matthew, Mark, and Luke: a Galilean phase, a journey, and a Jerusalem phase.

Often in the gospel narrative we do not have the words of Jesus so much as the Christian communities' affirmation and understanding of the power of Jesus which was read into words attributed to him.

To get to the episode you mentioned, Rabbi Spiro, it is certainly a fact that either Jesus claimed the power to forgive sin, or the Christian community claimed it for him. Your question is: What was the authority for that claim? The Christian would answer that Jesus was his own authority. We would beg the reader of the gospel not to translate *sin* as an evil deed, so that *forgiveness* would mean "divine pardon." Rather, sin must be understood as the manifestation of a broken, distorted, inadequately loved life, for then forgiveness has a totally different meaning. The power that overcomes sin or that forgives sin is the power of love that goes beneath the external deed level of our behavior and embraces, accepts, and affirms our being, calling us thereby into the fullness of life. In this state of forgiveness, we can celebrate our being. At the deepest level, forgiveness, acceptance, and love are synonymous. The one who has experienced this gift manifests it by forgiving himself, accepting himself, loving himself, and being himself without apology for his weakness and without boasting of his talents.

The Christian affirmation about Jesus is that in him and through him the love of God broke into life with a new intensity, restoring God's creation to its fullness. When the guilt of our inadequacy confronts this power of love, we experience forgiveness. That is the basis of the claim, made either by Jesus or for Jesus, that he has the power to forgive sin because he has the power to bring to humanity the life-giving love of God.

RABBI SPIRO: Is it possible to limit anti-Semitism or anti-Judaism if passages such as the following from the Book of John continue to be read and studied and believed?

"After these things, Jesus walked in Galilee, for he would not walk in Jewry because the Jews sought to kill him."

And there are other New Testament references of a pejorative and derogatory nature about Jews.

MR. SPONG: I do not plead innocent to the charges that Christians have, through the ages, been guilty of giving birth to and nourishing anti-Semitism. I regret it. As a Christian, I apologize for it. It is not a noble chapter in our history. The reasons for it are all too human. Christianity was born from the womb of Judaism, and we grew up to leave our parent and our home. As with every adolescent, the leaving of parental domination is accompanied somewhat by hostile feelings. In the early years of their history, Christians were the victims of Jewish persecution; but following the fall of Jerusalem in A.D. 70, the Jewish-Christian population and influence diminished in the life of the Church and so too did the threat of persecution at the hands of the Jews. Their struggle was no longer with the Jews but with the Roman Empire. Unfortunately, the scars and the ill feelings of that first struggle lingered. Much of the first century Christian writing reflects the earlier hostility and sets it in concrete for all eternity where it can constantly feed the baser instincts of our humanity, exacerbating our prejudices.

The fact is that the challenge of Jesus and the death of Jesus occurred in a Jewish context. The executors, according to the narratives, were the Roman authorities; but they executed at the behest of the Jewish hierarchy. The meaning of Jesus and his message were rejected by some Jewish people but not because these people were bad or evil. The first Christians were also Jews, we must remember, who saw in Jesus the revelation of Yahveh himself. According to the Book of Acts, the first Gentile convert to Christianity was some years later. However, there were among the Jewish people both those who embraced this Christ and those who rejected him. Our first struggle was a civil war between believing Jews and nonbelieving Jews. Far from portraying them as the unbelievers, we should be aware that the Jews were the only people who could possibly have understood and responded to this Christ. These people were the children of a heritage of religious genius and deep insight. They were the most God-intoxicated nation on the face of the earth. Instead of persecuting Jews for the death of the one we call our Lord, we ought to give thanks that they and they alone could have given us this Jesus.

However, to deal with your question specifically, the gospel from which you quoted is, on the surface, the most anti-Semitic, but that is to misread that gospel. John is generally dated about A.D. 110 and is, therefore, the last gospel to be written. This was well after the fall of Jerusalem and the subsequent decline of

Jewish power in both the world and the Church. It was written for a Gentile audience in the midst of a controversy with the people called "Gnostics," who wanted to spiritualize Christianity in a Greek nonworldly direction. John chose to symbolize all of those people who, though close to the grace of God, were blind to its power and meaning with the term "the Jews"; but for John that term included Gentiles and Gnostics as well as Jews.[2] Therefore, in the fourth gospel the title "the Jews" does not necessarily mean an ethnic or racial group. It means those who cannot see or respond or understand among all the human race. It was, however, an unfortunate choice of words with an evil and ugly connotation in history that we cannot undo.

We can, however, through such experiences as this dialogue, seek to sensitize one another to our blind spots. We can attempt to stem that tide of prejudice that warps and kills not only the victim but also the one who harbors the prejudice. Whether prejudice be religious or racial, it is a sickness that needs the strong medicine of both judgment and healing. In human experience, when a child completes his adolescent rebellion and hostility and grows into maturity, he looks again at his parents with a new love and appreciation. Judaism is the mother of Christianity. It has the wisdom of the ages; it has given us our Lord and our life. You, our Jewish brothers and sisters, deserve the payment of the infinite debt of gratitude that we Christians owe you. Perhaps in this generation we may have the grace to approach each other in love and appreciation. Nothing less than that is worthy of either the children of Abraham or the disciples of the Christ.

RABBI SPIRO: How would you respond to Jewish children who are told that they are "Christ-killers"?

MR. SPONG: I am pained at the thought that a follower of Jesus would vent his own neurotic hate on a Jewish child in such a manner, for that is what it is. Again, I am sorry it happens; and yet I know that it does. It exhibits the same mentality that segregates blacks and feeds racial bigotry. It is certainly not true to the meaning of the one we claim to serve.

Jesus was never vindictive. His response even to his persecutors was to love them, accept them, and forgive them. Since he did not view life on the level of deeds, it would be inconceivable that he could condone an attitude that would blame a child in today's generation for the misunderstanding of a historic ancestor. Such a concept reveals only a distorted mind. To a child who is victimized by the irrational charge, "Christ-killer," I say, pray for that person whose mind is so twisted and whose spirit is so sick that he mutters his own warped words and reveals thereby only the depth of his own self-hatred.

RABBI SPIRO: Do you think that Christians should try to convert Jews to Christianity?

MR. SPONG: I think that Christians should be Christians. We are called to live out our gospel by loving, accepting, and forgiving one another. We should be agents of life, calling everyone we meet into a deeper awareness of and sensitivity to genuine humanity. If, in the process of doing that, someone should ask the Christian to tell him or her about the source of this love, then it is appropriate for a Christian to share the content of his faith, as one would share any personal treasure with a friend. To impose the Christian story on one's hearer when it is not requested is the height of arrogance and a violation of the human integrity of another child of God. Inevitably, any attempt at conversion will invest Christianity with the not-so-subtle judgment that all but Christians are inferior and that Christians alone possess the truth. When we Christians act that way, we are not following our Lord; we are only seeking to meet the insecurity needs of our neurosis. We are being imperialistic out of our desire to prove our worth and our superiority. We are doing violence to the power of our Christ, who is recognized not in words or creeds or sacred formulas but in the life, love, being, freedom, and wholeness of those who have experienced his power.

In this Jewish-Christian dialogue, for example, I have become a more deeply committed and more sensitive Christian. I trust that Rabbi Spiro has become a more deeply committed and more sensitive Jew. I hope that both of us have embraced our humanity a little more fully and expanded our consciousness of life to a new dimension. I know that I have made many friends who enrich my life greatly. I rejoice in that and am free to love you in your Jewishness; and I pray that you will love me in my Christianity. My hope is that we will learn to listen to the depth of truth that each of us holds and be open to the constant nudging of God that each of us experiences. St. John says that if we abide in love, we will abide in God. I am content with that truth, even though I will continue to call him Christ or Holy Trinity, and you will continue to call him Yahveh.

So be it.

Shalom to you, my brothers and sisters.

NOTES

1. If the reader wanted an outline, I think the scenes would look like this.

scene 1	The temple	Luke 1:5–25
scene 2	Nazareth	Luke 1:26–38
scene 3	Judah	Luke 1:39–56
scene 4	John's birth	Luke 1:57–80
scene 5	The journey to Bethlehem	Luke 2:1–7
scene 6	The hillside, moving to the stable	Luke 2:8–21
scene 7	The circumcision and the presentation	Luke 2:21–38
scene 8	The Bar Mitzvah	Luke 2:39–52

2. Edwyn C. Hoskyns, *The Fourth Gospel*, vol. 2 (Faber & Faber, Ltd., 1939), p. 16.

chapter VI

CHRISTIAN GIFTS TO JUDAISM

The dialogue concluded in the synagogue as Jews sought to acknowledge and embrace their debt to Christians.

Rabbi Judah ben Ezekiel is recorded in the Talmud as saying that if a person sees trees in blossom he should pronounce a benediction. Our tree of dialogue has borne the fruit of understanding and the blossoms of mutual respect.

During the dialogue, Mr. Spong stated that the history of Christian-Jewish relations has not been good. I would have to agree with him when I recall such episodes as the Spanish Inquisition, the various expulsions of Jews, the European Crusades, and the pogroms staged in the name of Jesus. Our history is not good; the past is not a source of pride, just as it is not a wellspring of compassion.

However, in spite of the dark veil of history, we can still be grateful as Jews for the contributions that Christians have made to Judaism. Rarely do we hear of such gifts. We do hear, perhaps too frequently, about oppression and discrimination through the centuries. We do hear, as Mr. Spong recalled, about the many contributions that Judaism, the "mother-religion," has made to Christianity, the "daughter-religion." We also hear about our similarities in the context of general values and abstract principles. But Judaism's debt to Christianity is a subject whose neglect is virtually complete.

We can go back into Jewish sources to see that the idea is not a new one. During the twelfth century, Moses Maimonides, known in Hebrew as "Rambam" and judged the greatest of all Jewish philosophers, reminded his fellow Jews in the *Mishneh Torah* that the teachings of Jesus "serve the purpose of preparing the way for the messiah, who is sent to make the whole world perfect by worshipping God with one spirit. For they have," he continued, "spread the words of the Bible and the law of truth over the wide globe. . . ."

Another important philosopher, Judah Halevi, who lived in the eleventh century, pointed out in his book, *The Kuzari*, that Judaism must take issue with the trinity and with the story of Jesus' birth. But like Maimonides, he went on to say that Christianity does contribute the preparatory steps to the messianic age which adherents of the three monotheistic faiths—Judaism, Christianity, and Islam—will share.

Joseph Yaabetz, a victim of Spanish persecution and a seminal thinker, believed that the Jewish people would have become weakened in their own faith were it not for the presence of Christians who served, through their own ideas and practices, as reminders of Jewish obligations. He makes a good point. If Judaism throughout the dispersion had been surrounded by nothing but pagan rites and heathen beliefs, it might have succumbed. But because Jews had a sister religion capable of spreading its branches wherever Jews lived, we were sheltered in many ways from the storms of paganism that might have blown us into oblivion.

A great thinker of the eighteenth century, Jacob Emden, wrote that Christians "will receive reward from God for having propagated a belief in him among nations that never heard his name."

I concur with these brilliant theologians of Jewish tradition: the world *has* been largely Judaized through Christianity. The Jewish message has been carried to the jungles of Africa, the tropics of South America, the glaciered lands of northern Europe. It is the Jewish message indelibly inscribed in the words of Isaiah that Christians have carried and transmitted throughout the world. This Hebrew prophet gave to his people a message that spelled out clearly and dramatically their divine vocation, their mission as a people. Speaking in God's name, he declared: "I have put my spirit upon [Israel]. He shall make the right to go forth to the nations . . . to go forth according to the truth. He shall not fail nor be crushed, till he have set the right in the earth. And the isles shall wait for his teaching" (42:1,3–4). Inspired by his God, the prophet realized that the restoration of Israel itself after the Babylonian exile was not enough for the Jewish people as their divine mission, as the transcendent purpose of their existence. No, God would also give them "for a light to the nations" so that his salvation and glory might extend unto the end of the earth (49:6).

But we could not and we *did* not accomplish this lofty mission by ourselves. The northern kingdom was obliterated by the onslaught of Assyrian forces. The southern kingdom was exiled by Babylonian troops. We were partially restored but greatly weakened. Later the Romans practically destroyed us, burning our temple and annihilating the capital city of Jerusalem. How could we sing our song in a foreign land, much less spread the message of Yahveh to the world? How could we be a light to the nations of the earth, or sound a clarion call of victory and strength to all peoples everywhere? No, the message of Judaism, a message of universal dimensions, might have been secluded in tribal oblivion had it not been for Christians who accepted the ambitious ideas of the prophet and spread them to the four corners of the world.

The best example of the results of this effort is the Hebrew Bible. Whether read or not, it still remains a best seller year after year. Millions of copies are sold annually. The Hebrew Bible, namely the Old Testament, has been translated into more than a thousand languages and dialects. What would have happened to it without its acceptance and transmission by Christianity? The very fact that it is available to millions of people to read and ponder, that its influence is truly universal, is one of the greatest contributions that Christianity has made to Judaism, actualizing the biblical hope that "out of Zion shall go forth the Torah and the word of Yahveh from Jerusalem" (Isa. 2:3). Because of Christianity, the message of the covenant between God and man, the idea of Israel's mission, and the code of ethical obligations have become universalized.

Judaism is also indebted to Christianity for propagating the Jewish idea of a God who is both loving and just. As the prophet Hosea stood before his people in Israel, he reminded them that their God Yahveh was a compassionate, forgiving, merciful God, a God who sought their return to him. Just as Hosea was willing to take back his wayward wife, so Yahveh was always ready to accept his people in love and mercy.

However, Hosea's ideas were qualified by Amos' idea of divine justice. Although unpopular and even endangered, Amos was undaunted in preaching his fiery message to his people: "Let justice well up as waters and righteousness as a mighty stream" (5:24).

Another prophet, Micah, saw the importance of joining the attributes of love and justice. Yahveh could not be understood or obeyed exclusively either as a God of justice or as a God of love; indeed, one attribute was as indispensable as the other. "It has been told you," exclaimed Micah, "what is good: only to do justice and to love mercy and to walk humbly before God" (6:8). We learn that justice must be tempered with mercy in order for mankind to live in dignity. As justice is impossible without mercy, so a world of mercy alone would be chaotic without the application of justice.

The author of the Book of Jonah makes a case for the inseparable combination ·of justice and mercy when, in his narrative, Jonah leaves his own land to bring the idea of a just and loving God to another civilization. Similarly, Christianity took this message for its own and brought it to other peoples.

Christianity also carried the priceless gift of the one, universal God, a gift that shocked, inspired, and transformed many peoples who had conceived of many or no gods. Prior to Judaism in Palestine and to Christianity throughout the rest of the world, monotheism—the belief in one God active in the universe and in the historic process—was unknown. When Christians accepted the idea of one God, even though manifested in the trinity, how the God of Israel grew! He became the

God that Isaiah and Jeremiah dreamed about as they preached in their own tiny land among their own people. They conceived of God as universal, but their idea was only an imaginative dream until Christianity made the dream a forceful reality throughout the world. We are indebted to Christians for universalizing the God of Israel, for making the prophetic dream come true.

In a world of amoral polytheism, of many gods competing for various privileges and powers, it is hard, if not impossible, to develop universal standards of conduct and unitary ideas about the nature and purpose of man. Through the one God of Israel, the Hebrews of biblical times were able to develop a view of man created in the divine image of God. It was a lofty, noble thought which carried with it the promise and even the demand that every human being must devote his efforts to becoming more and more human. Through the commandments, the *mitzvot* of the Torah, we are to emulate the ethical image of God himself. "Be holy, for I, the Lord your God, am holy" (Lev. 19:2). So Jews conceived and believed in the perfectibility of man, a rare concept in the world of paganism and polytheism. Thanks to Christianity, this noble image of man has become an important legacy throughout the world.

Realizing the ultimate goals that we try to achieve as human beings created in God's image, we also recognize our responsibility to help others whose human potential may be lost or obscured. Christianity, especially through the writings of the New Testament, reminds us clearly and trenchantly that we must work with the sinner, the degenerate, the criminal, the downcast, the forgotten. They are our brothers, although their divine image appears dimmed by overwhelming troubles. Cain asked God, "Am I my brother's keeper?" Christianity answered by unfolding a theology not only of faith but also of good works among all men, however downtrodden, however crushed and abject. We are our brother's keeper—our desperate, depressed, disconsolate brother as well as our affluent and comfortable brother. How forcefully Christianity drives this home for all of us to share, exemplified most selflessly in the adage of the

Salvation Army: "A man may be down but he's never out."

A professor of mine once said that the entire corpus of prophetic literature in the Bible can be summed up in one statement by Isaiah: "Give rest to the weary" (28:12). Christianity has made this prophetic admonition the heart and soul of its social gospel. When a person is in the depths of poverty, when he feels that the whole world has crumbled upon him, when he feels crushed by the brutal weight of famine and despair, then he is weary. Our task is to give him rest, to relieve him of his pain in the weariness of despair.

This message is the golden rule of Christianity, reminding us that there is a covenant not only between God and man, but also between man and man. Indeed, if the human covenant is not realized, then the divine covenant is empty of power and purpose.

But we must go beyond the theology of the New Testament and the global mission of Christianity for our indebtedness as Jews. We are also indebted as a minority group living in this great country. As Jews, we have been persecuted, expelled, and gassed; we have been slaughtered *en masse* and maligned; we have been accused falsely of the most bestial crimes; and we have been subject to every indignity and cruelty the human imagination has conceived. Yet one of the greatest gifts we have ever received in any country has been, and is, the first amendment of the United States Constitution. This assures us the right to worship and to live openly as Jews, not with condescending acceptance, but with total freedom as human beings. Congress shall make no laws establishing a religion nor prohibiting the free exercise of religion. Religious freedom is a guarantee, a right without qualification in this country. We are protected as Jews because we are accepted as full and equal citizens. I mention this as an important facet of our indebtedness because after much struggle and many obstacles, our founding fathers who framed the Bill of Rights were successful. And our country's founding fathers were Christians! Without this guarantee of religious freedom, how could Jews have survived at all in the United States? We were not able to survive anywhere else for very long without being victimized by persecution or expulsion or both. We have not only survived but prospered as Jewish citizens of the United States because our Christian brethren struggled to give every citizen the God-given right to be free in every respect. Having fully accepted this gift with immeasurable gratitude, we Jews must work with Christians as each other's keepers to preserve it zealously, to guard it vigilantly.

Jew and Christian . . . we have been through so much together during the past two millennia. We have fought against each other and with each other. We have been maligned and misunderstood from both sides. We have rarely opened up to understand each other. Seldom have we understood that we need not sacrifice our own identities and our own legacies by talking with each other. On the contrary, Jewish identity is affirmed and strengthened through the glorious power of open, free, honest communication. I realize who I am, as a Jew, more clearly by understanding more intelligently who my Christian neighbor is. Aided by communication and secure in the mutual appreciation of our respective traditions, no longer must I worry about which is the superior religion. We are indebted to each other as we both strive, in the context of our own distinctive customs and beliefs, to fulfill in our lives and throughout the world the love and righteousness of the one God.

Back in the twelfth century, Don Pedro, king of Aragon, was confused about Judaism and Christianity. The king, of course, was a Christian. He had heard of a wise Jew in his land whose name was Ephraim Sancho, and he asked that Ephraim be brought to him.

When Ephraim arrived before Don Pedro's throne, the king asked: "Which faith is superior, yours or mine?" When Ephraim heard the king's question, he was thrown into confusion. He said: "Our faith, O King, suits us better, for when we were slaves in Egypt, our God, by means of many wondrous miracles, led us out of bondage into freedom. For you Christians, however, your own faith is the better because by it you have been able to establish your rule over most of the earth."

When Don Pedro heard this he was angered and said: "I didn't ask you what benefits each religion brings to its believers. What I want to know is, which is superior—yours or mine?"

Again Ephraim was troubled. He thought to himself: "If I tell the king that his religion is superior to mine, I will have denied the God of my fathers, and I'll truly deserve all the punishments of eternity. On the other hand, should I tell him that my religion is better than his, he will be sure to burn me at the stake."

To the king, Ephraim said: "If it please the king, let me ponder his majesty's question for three days, because it requires much reflection. At the end of the third day I will come with my answer."

King Pedro said: "Let it be as you say."

For the three days that followed, the spirit of Ephraim was torn within him. He neither ate nor slept but put on sackcloth and ashes and prayed for divine guidance. But when the time arrived for him to see the king, he put all fear aside and went to the palace with his answer. When he came before the king, he looked downcast.

"Why are you so sad?" the king asked him.

Ephraim replied: "I am sad with good reason because without any cause whatsoever I was humiliated today. Please be my judge in this matter, O King."

"Speak!" said Don Pedro.

Ephraim Sancho then began: "A month ago to this day a neighbor of mine, a jeweler, went on a distant journey. Before he departed, in order to preserve the peace between his two sons while he was away, he gave each of them a gift of a costly gem. Only today the two brothers came to me and said: 'Ephraim, give us the values of these gems and judge which is the superior of the two.'

"I replied: 'Your father himself is a great artist and an expert on precious stones. Why don't you ask him? Surely he will give you a better judgment than I.'

"When they heard this they became enraged. They abused me. O King, judge whether or not my grievance is just."

The king shouted: "Those rogues have mistreated you without cause! They deserve to be punished for this outrage!"

When Ephraim Sancho heard the king speak in this way he rejoiced. "O King," he said, "your words are true and just. Each brother received a priceless gem. You have asked me, O King, which of the two gems is superior. How can I give you a proper answer? Send a messenger to the only expert of these gems—the one God of the Universe. Let him tell you which is the better."

I have mentioned many gifts that we have given to each other as Jews and Christians through the centuries. The greatest of these is the gift of each other.

chapter VII

TWO FESTIVALS OF LIGHT

Together we sought the inner power of our winter festivals, Hanukah and Christmas.

In the year 175 B.C., a new king assumed the throne of the Seleucid Empire, which included Palestine. His name was Antiochus IV. He chose as his royal title the name Epiphanes, hardly a modest claim, for it literally means "the revealed God."

Antiochus Epiphanes was a Syrian. He was part of the ruling elite of the Macedonian empire which had dominated the world since its conquest of Greece in the fourth century before the birth of Jesus. That empire was marked by immense military power, but it was also characterized by vast cultural power. Everywhere that the empire of Macedonia moved, it carried with it the beauties of Greek civilization—the art, the language, and the concepts of the Greek world became universal. So dominant was this culture that when the armies of Rome defeated the Macedonians in battle in the first century B.C., it was the culture of Macedonia that overwhelmed that of Rome. This situation continued for three hundred years into the Roman era. This meant that in A.D. 56, when Paul wrote a letter to the Christians living in Rome, the capital of the empire, he wrote in Greek rather than Latin, for Greek was the language that the citizens of Rome used. The culture of Hellas had mastered Greece's military conqueror.

There was in the Macedonian world tremendous cultural pride that bordered on snobbery. Everything Hellenistic was considered superior. Everything non-Hellenistic was quite inferior, so the dominant thrust of the empire was to Hellenize the world. Hellenistic dress, manners, sports, life style, and worship became the vogue for everyone. In the path of this process, local customs were abandoned and demolished. In city after city the leading citizens among the conquered people rushed to emulate their "superior" conquerors.

This was also true in the tiny conquered province of Judah. Many Jews seemed eager to abandon their Hebrew heritage, blending in with the dominant mood of Hellenism. Their Hebrew loyalties waned, and Hebrew worship languished.

The king, Antiochus Epiphanes, sensing this mood, sought to accelerate it. He envisioned a universal people where all differences were blurred and culture was the single unifying force of the empire. He was successful in buying the loyalty of the Jerusalem high priest, a man named Jason. Finally, Antiochus reduced Jason to a complete puppet. Then, having no further need of him, Antiochus removed Jason from his priestly position. In his boldest and most arrogant act yet, Antiochus appointed Menelaus to be the high priest of Judah, a man who was not even in the priestly tradition.

Menelaus had no claim to the priestly office. He had no training and no preparation; he was not even a believing, practicing Jew. Antiochus' plan was to remove Judaism from Judah, and with the appointment of Menelaus that removal was to come at the hand of one who wore the symbolic vestments of the high priest. It was an insidious plot; and some Jews, eager to be done with their Jewishness, applauded that decision.

Next, Antiochus Epiphanes ordered that the temple of Judah be stripped of every vestige of Judaism. Jewish cultic symbols were removed; and a statue of Zeus, a Greek god, was installed in the Jewish holy of holies. With every new order from Antiochus, the pagan high priest, Menelaus, complied with increasing glee.

At that moment Judaism could have ceased to be a living force. It was in danger of becoming merely a footnote in the history books of antiquity. This ancient and noble tradition literally hung by a thread. Had that thread snapped, the worship of Israel which kept Jews separate from the world, would have disappeared. The Jewish people would have lost their reason for being, and all of those things to which Judaism was later to give birth—including Christianity—would have ceased to be historic possibilities. That was a crisis moment for Judaism, but in retrospect we see it as a crisis moment in the history of the world.

Into that breach, one man dared to enter, raising his voice in defiance. His name was Mattathias; and he called to the people of Yahveh to stand up, to bear witness, to fight, to die if need be, in order to preserve the light that they had discovered in the God of their fathers.

Mattathias had five sons. One of them, whose name was Judas, organized a rag-tag army of Jewish volunteers into an effective guerrilla force that dealt so many stinging blows to the army of Antiochus Epiphanes that Judas was given the nick-name *Maccabaeus*, which means "the hammer"—Judas the Hammer. His military exploits are written in the books of the Apocrypha called First and Second Maccabees.

Finally, after three years of guerrilla tactics, Judas Macca-baeus lured the army of Antiochus Epiphanes into a trap and routed his foes. That battle took place in the height of winter, and because of it Judaism was saved. The guerrilla force of Judas Maccabaeus marched into Jerusalem. They entered their temple, purging all the pagan symbols and influences; and they lighted an oil lamp to Yahveh in the darkness of their reclaimed sanctuary. That lamp burned for eight days while they cele-brated with songs and dances and prayers.

Judas Maccabaeus enjoined upon Jewish people of all time the annual dedicatory observance of this moment when the light of true worship returned to the temple of the Lord. Thus the Jewish festival of lights was born. We call it *Hanukah*. In Jewish homes across this land, Hanukah begins with the lighting of the first candle in the eight-branched candelabra called the meno-rah. Hanukah recalls a holy and crucial moment in history—a moment that Christians can share with Jews, for in the success of Judas Maccabaeus in 165 B.C. the destiny of both Christians and Jews was preserved.

Hanukah can also be a holy period for Christians, for it celebrates the light of true worship once more shining in the darkness of human distortion. Because of the proximity in time of Hanukah to Christmas, there has been a gentle blending of the two holidays, so that Hanukah is even sometimes called "the Jewish Christmas." Hanukah is marked by recognizable Christmas customs: decorated houses, the exchange of gifts, the sending of cards.

There is a deeper connection and a greater similarity uniting Hanukah and Christmas, however, and we must explore this in order to develop a full and mutual appreciation. Both Hanukah and Christmas come in the dead of winter. Both use light as a major symbol. Both speak to the ancient hopes of human beings that truth will banish falsehood and that light will banish darkness.

Among our primitive human ancestors, the approach of the winter solstice gripped their lives with shivering fear. Our ancient, almost prehistoric, ancestors did not understand the planets' relationship to the sun and the cyclical nature of the seasons. They could only watch with anxiety as the days grew shorter and shorter and the nights, so filled with terror for our forebears, grew longer and longer. They literally wondered if light itself were passing out of existence. Then there came that day when the light stopped its relentless retreat and began to come back—a day barely noted in our scientific world as the shortest day in the year, December 21. But for our ancient forefathers, that day was an occasion of immense relief, of wild celebration, and of divine worship.

It was in this way that light itself became a symbol for God, and so it is that in most major religions there is a holy day or a holy season that marks the coming of light into the darkness of winter. Hanukah is that holy time for Jews; Christmas is that holy season for Christians. So it is not surprising that Hanukah is called the "festival of lights," nor is it surprising that the Christmas story is told with stars shining in a black sky and with angelic choruses and heavenly light splitting the darkness of night. Jesus is called by Christians the "light of lights," "a light to lighten the Gentiles"; and John has him say, "I am the light of the world."

Hanukah is the Jewish way of saying that light pushes back darkness when true worship is restored to the temple of Judah, for it is in the worship of Judaism that Jewish people find their ultimate truth.

Christmas is the Christian way of saying that light pushes back darkness when the love of God is born in human history. For it is in the love that created life in Jesus of Nazareth that Christians find their ultimate truth.

It is human to search for the light of truth. All of us do it. When that light is found, we seek to live in its power until we find ourselves aglow with its flame. Then, taking that experience of light, we give it content; and it becomes our revelation, our tradition, and our truth. Hanukah is that for the Jews; Christmas is that for Christians. The content is different; the revelation is different; the tradition is different. But we can see in both Christianity and Judaism a common yearning, a common humanity, and a common hope. We believe that behind the diverse traditions of men there is a common God who calls us all to come to him by whatever path we dare to walk.

Have we not all one Father?
Did not one God create us?
[MALACHI 2:10]

BIBLIOGRAPHY

ALLPORT, GORDON W. *The Nature of Prejudice.* Doubleday Anchor Book, 1958.

BAUM, GREGORY. *The Jews and the Gospel.* Newman Press, 1961.

BROWN, RAYMOND E. *Gospel According to John.* Doubleday, 1970.

DE CORNEILLE, ROLAND. *Christians and Jews.* Harper & Row, Publishers, 1966.

DIMONT, MAX. *Jews, God, and History.* The New American Library, 1962.

EAKIN, FRANK E., JR. *The Religion and Culture of Israel: An Introduction to Old Testament Thought.* Allyn and Bacon, Inc., 1971.

FLANNERY, EDWARD H. *The Anguish of the Jews.* The Macmillan Co., 1965.

GASTER, THEODOR H. *Festivals of the Jewish Year.* William Sloane Associates, 1953.

HAENCHEN, ERNST. *The Acts of the Apostles.* Westminster Press, 1971.

HOSKYNS, EDWYN C. *The Fourth Gospel.* Faber & Faber, Ltd., 1939.

JACOBS, LOUIS. *What Does Judaism Say About . . . ?* Quadrangle, 1973.

KERTZER, MORRIS N. *What is a Jew?* The Macmillan Company, 1971.

MINEAR, PAUL S. *The Interpreter and the Birth Narratives.* Wretmans Boktryckeri A.B., 1950.

PARKES, JAMES. *A History of the Jewish People.* Penguin Books, Inc., 1964.

ROBINSON, JOHN A. T. *The Human Face of God.* Westminster Press, 1973.

ROTH, CECIL. *A History of the Jews,* rev. ed. Schocken Books, 1970.

ROTH, LEON. *Judaism: A Portrait.* The Viking Press, 1961.

SANDMEL, SAMUEL. *We Jews and Jesus.* Oxford University Press, 1973.

SCHWARTZMAN, SYLVAN D. AND JACK D. SPIRO. *The Living Bible.* Union of American Hebrew Congregations, 1971.

SILVERMAN, WILLIAM B. *Rabbinic Wisdom and Jewish Values.* Union of American Hebrew Congregations, 1971.

SPONG, JOHN S. *Honest Prayer.* Seabury Press, 1973.
This Hebrew Lord. Seabury Press, 1974.

STEINBERG, MILTON. *Basic Judaism.* Harcourt, Brace, and Company, 1947.

VON RAD, GERHARD. *Genesis.* Westminster Press, 1972.